D0673964

THE BEGINNINGS
OF LIFE

*How Generation Follows Generation
in the Animal Kingdom*

CHRIS CATTON AND JAMES GRAY

DRAGON'S WORLD

A DRAGON'S WORLD BOOK

Dragon's World Ltd.
Limpsfield
Surrey RH8 0DY
Great Britain

First published by Dragon's World 1991

© Dragon's World Ltd., 1991

© Chris Catton and James Gray, 1991

All rights reserved.

No part of this book may be reproduced or
transmitted in any form or by any means,
electronic or mechanical, including
photocopying, recording, or by any
information storage and retrieval system,
without prior permission in writing from
Dragon's World Ltd., except by a reviewer
who may quote brief passages in a review.

Editor   Martyn Bramwell
Designer   Peter Ward
Picture Researcher Suzanne Williams
Editorial Director Pippa Rubinstein

**British Library
Cataloguing in Publication Data**
Catton, Chris
  The beginnings of life.
  1. Animals. Reproduction.
  I. Title II. Gray, James *1946 –*
  591.1'6

ISBN 1 85028 101 7

Frontispiece: **A harvest mouse in its nest.**

Photograph on pages 2/3: **Japanese red-crowned cranes
performing their elegant courtship dance in the late spring
snow.**

▶ **Male golden toads gather at a breeding pool
to await the arrival of females. This beautiful
Central American amphibian is now very rare,
and is officially listed as an endangered species.**

Typeset in Great Britain by
Action Typesetting Limited, Gloucester
Printed in Singapore

CONTENTS

WHY DO ANIMALS REPRODUCE?

An animal has to do a whole range of things in order to survive. It has to drink, breathe, grow, eat and avoid being eaten by other animals. But simply staying alive is not enough. One day, every individual must die, so animals have to have one other essential ability. They have to be able to replace themselves — to reproduce.

If an animal fails to reproduce, its kind will die out, and that goes for every one of the million or so types of animal that there are in the world. It is not surprising that with so many different species there are quite a variety of different ways of reproducing. Some animals lay eggs; others give birth to live young. There are animals that grow miniature copies of themselves out of their sides, and others that just split in half. The way an animal goes about making new generations of its own kind depends on how and where it lives, but just as importantly, its method of reproduction can affect many aspects of its own life. It can even determine how big the animal grows, or how colourful (or drab) it is.

▶ A walrus colony basks in the Sun on the rocky shore of Round Island, Alaska.

A Matter of Survival

For many people the most fascinating animals are humans, but there is a great deal to be learned about humans by studying other animals. To take just one example, many people who would otherwise have been childless can now be helped to have children of their own because studies of animal reproduction have helped us understand our own reproductive biology. We reproduce in virtually the same way as other mammals, and the only obvious difference is that we have fewer offspring than most. Yet in spite of this, our population is growing at a frightening rate.

The success of human reproduction can only be explained by the careful way we look after our children. We go on protecting and helping our offspring far longer than any other species. In most animals a very large proportion of the young die early in life. In some fishes, fewer than one in ten thousand survive to reach adulthood, and among the smaller sea creatures the death toll can be even higher. Compared with this, relatively few children die, even in the poorest human societies. By looking after our children so carefully we more than make up for our very low birth rate.

We humans are different in other ways too. For instance, it would be extremely foolish to try to understand human mating behaviour simply by comparing it with the way some other animal behaves. Male

Decisions

When thinking or writing about animals, it is often easier to work in shorthand, saying things like "an oyster's best strategy is to produce millions of eggs", as though the oyster thought about how many eggs it should produce, and planned its future. This is not the sort of decision that any oyster ever made, for the number of eggs an animal lays is the result of millions of years of evolution. Unfortunately, to avoid the shorthand means employing a lot of technical language. On balance the authors have decided to keep the shorthand where necessary, but remind readers that while animals may make real decisions about their choice of mate or their nest site, their evolutionary "decisions" are made through the process of natural selection and not through individual choice.

lions have several mates and let them do all the hunting, but this does not make it right for a man to have several women and spend all his time drinking. Humans are not lions, and our behaviour is not determined by the things that determine a lion's behaviour. The differences are just as important as any similarities. This point is conveniently forgotten by people (usually men) who like to argue that it is natural for a woman to do all the work of looking after her children because in most mammals it is the female who looks after the young. As we shall see later on, there are many species of mammal in which the male helps to raise the young, and it makes just as much sense (maybe more) to think that humans fall into this group.

The study of the ways in which animals reproduce may give us some clues about our own behaviour, but it is also important to remember that humans *think*. We make decisions that are much more complicated than those of even the most intelligent animals. It may be "natural" for humans to live in caves and beat off lions with sticks, but today we live in houses and apartment blocks, and take photographs of lions with cameras. Even if a study of human behaviour shows that a particular set of actions is perfectly normal and natural, that does not mean it is the way we *have* to behave. Unlike most other animals, human beings nearly always have a choice.

The giant panda – a species in danger

Pandas have a problem because they live entirely on bamboo. Every 80 years or so, large areas of bamboo flower and then die in the mountains of China where the animals live. Originally this was no great problem for pandas: when the bamboo died they could simply move to another area where there was bamboo of a different species for them to eat. But pandas are becoming rare in the wild because vast areas of their natural habitat have been destroyed. The surviving pockets of suitable bamboo forest are becoming so small and so isolated that it is impossible for the pandas to find new sources of bamboo when one patch dies out. This is a threat to individual pandas, but the biggest danger for pandas as a species is the fact that there are now so few animals left that it is becoming increasingly difficult for them to breed successfully. And if they fail to breed, they are certainly doomed.

◀ A North American bobcat closes in on a snowshoe hare, one of its main prey species. One day, every animal must die, whether from old age or in the claws or jaws of a predator. If animals did not reproduce, their species would very soon become extinct.

Growing Up

It would not take an intelligent creature visiting Earth from another planet very long to realize that humans, like most large animals on Earth, come in two sexes: male and female. Given time, the visitor would probably work out that the difference is to do with reproduction. It might take longer to realize that there are many animals that do not have sexes, but our visitor would surely understand that humans and other animals have to reach a certain age before they can reproduce. Animals cannot reproduce until they are mature, but the time it takes to reach maturity varies enormously for different species. Insects like flies can breed within days of hatching, for mice it takes a few weeks, and for humans it takes years.

▲ Most societies have some particular way of marking the time when children become adults. In the West it may be a special birthday party at 18 or 21, while for these Mehinacu girls in Brazil it will mean spending six months in a darkened hut, learning the mysteries of life and the tribe's social rules from the older women of the village.

Humans usually mature between the ages of about 11 and 17, but it is perfectly normal for some people to mature even earlier or later. Maturity is just the result of growing up, and there is nothing that can be done to speed it up or slow it down. As children start to mature, they usually put on an enormous spurt of growth. Girls generally mature earlier than boys, so girls between the ages of about 11 and 13 tend to be taller than boys of the same age.

As a girl matures into a woman, she changes in several ways. Her body changes shape as she develops breasts and her hips grow broader. Changes also happen inside her body. A woman's womb is the part of her body where a baby grows during pregnancy, and a girl's womb grows bigger as she matures. As a boy matures, his body grows bigger and more muscular. He grows a beard and his voice breaks, but

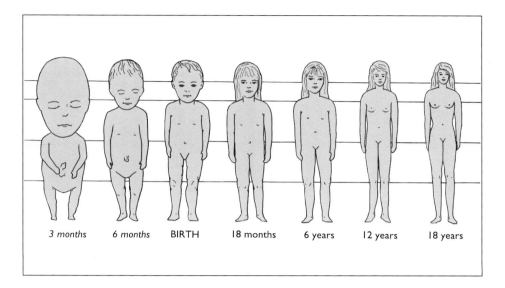

3 months   6 months   BIRTH   18 months   6 years   12 years   18 years

◀ The proportions of the human body change enormously throughout life. In a three-month embryo the head is as big as the body, and even at birth it is still large compared with the body and limbs. By two years old a child is just about half the height it will be as an adult, but its head is already three-quarters adult size.

▼ The diagrams below show the reproductive organs of the human male and female. The woman's bladder lies directly in front of the uterus (the womb), so in order to see the other organs clearly it has been drawn slightly to one side of its true position.

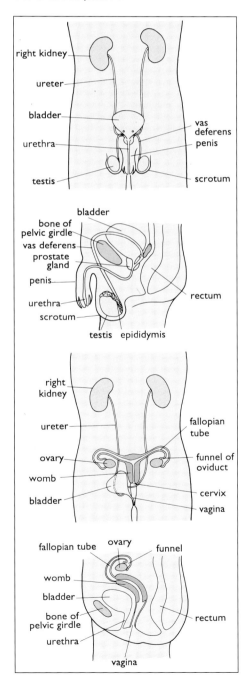

none of these changes makes it possible for the boy to become a father any more than the changes in the shape of a girl's body make it possible for her to be a mother.

A girl cannot become a mother until she begins to release eggs. These are tiny, about the size of a pin-head, and are made in the ovaries. A woman has two ovaries, one on either side of her womb, and they are connected to the womb by the fallopian tubes. When a baby girl is born, there are already 400,000 eggs in her ovaries. After reaching maturity, one of these eggs will be released each month and will then move down into her womb. As the egg is released, the womb changes slightly. It becomes larger, and the walls thicken, so as to be ready in case the egg is fertilized and a pregnancy begins.

If the woman does not become pregnant, all these preparations are wasted, and the extra lining of her womb peels off. This makes the womb bleed, and the blood passes down her birth canal or vagina producing what is known as her period. The egg is lost along with this blood, but a new one is soon released from the woman's ovaries, and she will have a period about every four weeks throughout her reproductive life, which usually lasts until she is about fifty years old.

The man's role in producing children consists of making sperm. These are even smaller than the eggs that a woman makes, and a man makes them by the billion. They are produced in the testes (testicles), two oval glands contained in a pouch of loose skin called the scrotum which hangs below and behind the penis. The function of the scrotum is to keep the testes at a lower temperature than the rest of the body as normal body temperature is too high for sperm storage. Fully developed sperm are carried along a pair of tubes which loop upward into the body and then join the base of the penis.

Once a girl's ovaries have started to release eggs and a boy's testes to produce sperm, physical maturity has been reached. At this point they may be quite capable of producing a baby, but most human societies recognize that there is more to being a good parent than simply producing a child. Everyone benefits if the parents are sufficiently experienced to cope with the demands of looking after a baby, and this is the main reason why young people are discouraged from producing babies and why most societies have laws and social rules that restrict the sexual freedom of young adults.

Pregnancy

In order to have children a woman must have a male partner, and in most human societies, but by no means all, she will have a free choice in selecting her mate. As with many other animals there is rarely any shortage of potential mates, but finding a man who is also willing and able to take on the responsibility of helping to feed, clothe, protect and educate a growing child is often more difficult. Different societies have different solutions to this problem, but almost every culture in the world has devised some sort of marriage ritual. By observing such a ritual the couple announce to each other, and to the rest of their society, that they intend to remain together and share the responsibility of raising any children they may have.

While marriage provides a social framework in which parents can raise their children it has nothing to do with the biological process of producing a baby. For a woman to become pregnant she needs to have intercourse with a man. During intercourse the man releases some of his sperm inside the woman's vagina, and from then on the contractions of the muscular walls of the vagina and uterus and the thrashing tails of the sperm propel the sperm up through the womb and into the fallopian tubes. If the woman is at the fertile stage of her monthly cycle and has recently released an egg, there is a chance that one of the sperm will succeed in fertilizing it.

As soon as a sperm comes into contact with the egg, the outer layer of the sperm's head-section peels away, and chemicals released by the sperm dissolve the jelly surrounding the egg. The sperm enters the egg, the nucleus joins with the nucleus of the egg, and as each nucleus is carrying a half-set of chromosomes, the newly fertilized egg has a complete set of instructions to control its growth and development.

Within hours of being fertilized, the egg starts to divide. It splits in half, then in half again, and each time it divides, the cells become smaller. At this stage the egg drifts freely in the fluid inside the mother's fallopian tube, and slowly it is pushed down the tube into the womb. It has no food supply, so there is no way for the tiny bundle of cells to grow; but by repeated splitting, the number of cells increases until eventually the bundle becomes a hollow ball of cells.

▶ The development of a human embryo occurs in stages. For the first few days the embryo is just a ball of cells. Then the ball folds in on itself, and different groups of cells start the process of developing into nerves, intestines, skin, bone and muscle cells. By about week 10 all the main parts of the body are recognizable, but it is not until about week 24 that the baby could possibly survive outside its mother's body, and even then it would require intensive medical care. Between week 24 and week 36 (the end of a full-term pregnancy) the baby roughly doubles its weight, which is why full-term babies are generally stronger and have a much better chance of survival than those that are born prematurely.

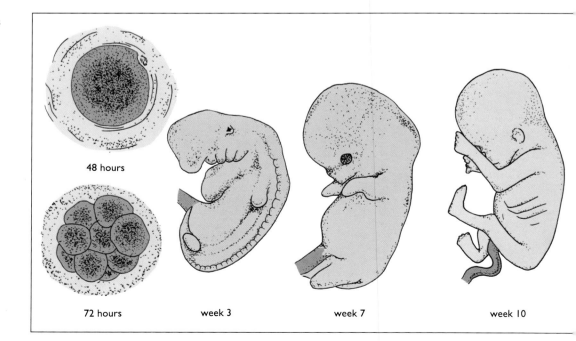

48 hours

72 hours   week 3   week 7   week 10

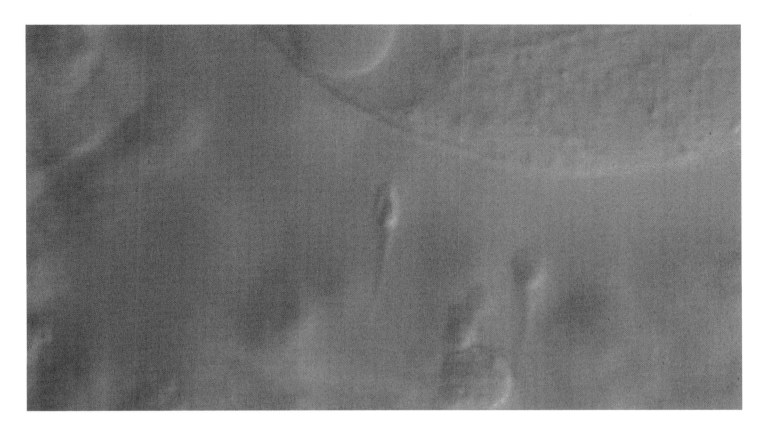

As the ball of cells develops it must also grow, and to do this it needs food. On about the sixth day after fertilization, the hollow ball becomes attached to the wall of the mother's womb. Cells on the surface of the ball begin to grow into the wall of the womb, and to absorb food from the mother's blood. Eventually these cells develop into the placenta – the baby's life support system – where a mass of blood vessels from the baby interlock with extra blood vessels that develop in the mother's womb. There is no direct flow of blood from mother to baby, but in the placenta food and oxygen pass from the mother's blood into the blood of the foetus, and waste material from the developing baby is carried safely away by the mother's blood.

▲ Only one of the many hundreds of sperm surrounding this human egg will succeed in fertilizing it. As soon as a single sperm has penetrated the thin surface layer and entered the egg, chemical changes occur in the cell wall which prevent any other sperm from entering.

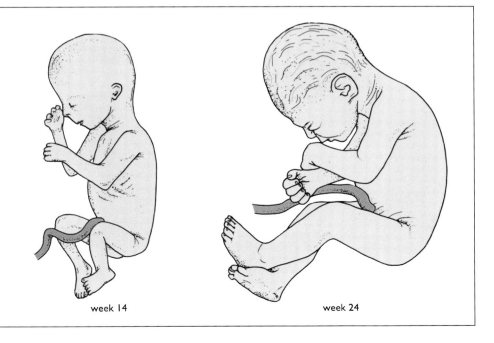

week 14   week 24

These major developments all happen within one month of an egg being fertilized, and it is usually at about this time that the woman begins to realize that she is pregnant. The first indication a woman gets that something has happened is that her period does not arrive when expected. When she is not pregnant, a woman has a period every month, but when she becomes pregnant, the placenta starts to produce two special hormones – chemicals that are released into the blood stream and act as messengers to other parts of the body. The hormones released from the placenta are called progesterone and oestrogen, and they do two things: they prevent the woman from having another period, and they prevent any more eggs being released from her ovaries. A side effect of these hormones is that they often make the woman feel sick, especially in the mornings, because they relax the muscles that close off the top of the stomach.

By the time the mother is aware that she is pregnant, her baby (at this stage called an embryo) is already well developed. During the early stages the embryo looks more like a tadpole than a human, but even at four weeks old it already has a heart, ears and eyes. By two months, the embryo has arms and legs and looks almost human. From about the fifteenth week onwards, the tissues of the embryo are all formed, and it simply has to grow. From about week 24 it might just be able to survive if it is born, but only with the help of modern medicine and technology. Babies are normally born about 38 weeks after the egg is fertilized, and in that time an embryo changes from being a single cell, barely visible to the naked eye, to a full-term human baby. It is the fastest period of growth and development in a human being's life.

"Test-tube babies"

In 1978 the first "test-tube baby" was born. Her name was Louise Brown, and she was the first person whose life did not start in the way described in the main text. Her mother could not become pregnant in the usual way because her fallopian tubes were blocked, but doctors were able to help. They took one of the eggs from Mrs Brown's body, and kept it in a laboratory. There, they placed it in a glass laboratory dish with some sperm from Mr Brown, and the egg was successfully fertilized. The doctors then put the fertilized egg back into Mrs Brown's womb, where it grew perfectly normally. Nine months later Louise was born.

It took many years of research before doctors found ways of keeping eggs and sperm alive

▲ Louise Brown celebrates her third birthday.

outside the parents' bodies and then getting the fertilized egg back into the womb so that it could develop into a normal baby. Since Louise's birth, doctors have been able to use this technique to help many people who were unable to have a baby in the normal way.

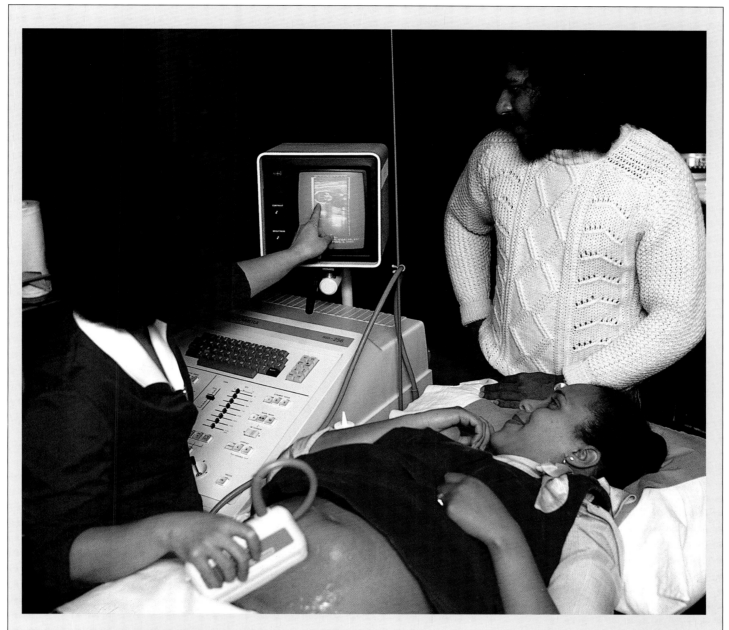

Amniocentesis

▲ The ultra-sound scanner beams very high frequency sound waves at the embryo in the womb and the echoes are analysed by computer to produce an image of the unborn baby.

Some babies are born with abnormalities that are caused by their genes. One of the commonest of these problems is known as Down's syndrome, and it leaves the baby handicapped. In normal babies, each cell contains two sets of chromosomes – one from the mother and one from the father. In babies with Down's syndrome, every cell has an extra copy of one chromosome so that instead of 46 chromosomes in each cell the Down's syndrome child has 47.

At present, nothing can be done to cure Down's syndrome or inherited conditions like it, but a breakthrough in modern medicine has made it possible to find out about an embryo's chromosomes before it is born. This is done by carefully removing a small amount of the amniotic fluid which surrounds the embryo in the womb. There are cells from the embryo in this fluid, and by examining them it is possible to see the chromosomes. One too many chromosomes, caused by the cell having an extra copy of chromosome number 21, indi-cates that the child will develop Down's syndrome. The method is also useful for identifying other genetic disorders. There are fierce arguments over whether or not it is right to make decisions for unborn children, but in most countries doctors will help a mother to end her pregnancy if the foetus is seriously abnormal and if this is what she wants. By looking at the chromosomes a doctor can also tell the sex of a child, but many parents do not want to know that before they find out at the moment of birth.

The Moment of Birth

A normal pregnancy lasts about nine months, and after that time the baby is ready to be born. The slight swelling of early pregnancy has now grown into a large bulge, and when the time eventually comes for the mother to give birth it is usually quite a relief for her.

Throughout pregnancy the placenta has been producing hormones, which prevent the woman from having a period. Obviously it would be disastrous for the baby if the mother had a period during pregnancy because the baby would be lost. But towards the end of pregnancy, the placenta and the womb begin to respond to new hormones being released by the foetus. These hormones cause the placenta and the womb to begin manufacturing a different group of hormones known as prostaglandins, and it is the prostaglandins that trigger the baby's birth.

Some time before birth, the baby usually turns round so that it has its head pointing downward inside the womb. The definite sign that the mother is about to give birth is when she starts to feel the muscles of her womb squeezing the baby downward. This contraction of the womb can be very uncomfortable for her, and for several hours she must suffer "labour pains" as the contractions grow stronger and more frequent. Eventually, the contractions squeeze the baby out of the womb, through the vagina or birth canal. The baby is usually born head first, although quite a few babies arrive feet first. When this happens the birth is known as a "breech" birth, and it usually takes a bit longer. Some babies are born in two or three hours, but for others the process can take up to 24 hours or even longer.

When the baby is born it is still attached to the placenta by the umbilical cord, so this has to be cut and tied up. The cut end heals quickly, producing the baby's navel. At the other end of the cord is the placenta, which is now useless. The placenta follows the baby down the birth canal, which is why it is known as the "afterbirth".

Giving birth is almost always a painful process for the mother, but mothers generally describe it as the most powerful experience of their lives. For the new mother lying exhausted, holding her newborn baby, it is the end of an ordeal, but it is also the beginning of the long-term commitment of parenthood.

▶ Giving birth is nearly always a painful and exhausting process for the mother, yet the moment of birth is also one of the most rewarding experiences life has to offer.

▶▶ Nestling against its mother's breast this six-week-old baby feels warm, safe and secure, and in addition to being the perfect nourishing baby food, the mother's milk contains antibodies that will help to protect the infant's body against infection.

Boy or Girl?

Henry VIII, the English Tudor King, was desperate for a son and heir: so desperate, in fact, that in his attempt to find a wife who would bear him a male child he ended up becoming famous for the ruthless way in which he rid himself of his "failed" wives. Of the six, he divorced two, beheaded two, one died after giving birth to his only male child and just one, Catherine Parr, outlived him. All this was because he firmly believed that no woman could ever run the country. But in this, as in other things, he was to be proved wrong. Although he did have a son,

▶ Henry VIII ruled England from 1509 to 1547, and like most people in the sixteenth century he believed that it was the woman who decided the sex of the children she bore. He was quite wrong – a child's sex is decided solely by the father – but Henry's desire for male heirs changed English history. In his search for a wife who would bear him sons he beheaded two wives and divorced two more. When the Church of Rome opposed the divorces, Henry declared the Church of England independent – and so started the Reformation.

it was his daughter Elizabeth who was destined to become one of England's most famous and successful monarchs.

Like all his court physicians, Henry believed that it was the woman who decided the sex of her child, and that therefore it was entirely the fault of his wives that they kept bearing him daughters. We now know that it is the man's sperm that is responsible. A man's sperm consists of two types, and they are produced in equal quantities. One type will produce girls, the other will produce boys, and it is purely a matter of chance which type fertilizes any particular egg.

Had Henry VIII been living today he would not have needed to wait until the child was born in order to discover whether it was a boy or girl. By taking a small sample of the fluid surrounding the developing baby and examining it closely, a doctor can tell the sex of the unborn child. The sex is actually decided at the moment when the sperm fertilizes the egg, nine months before birth.

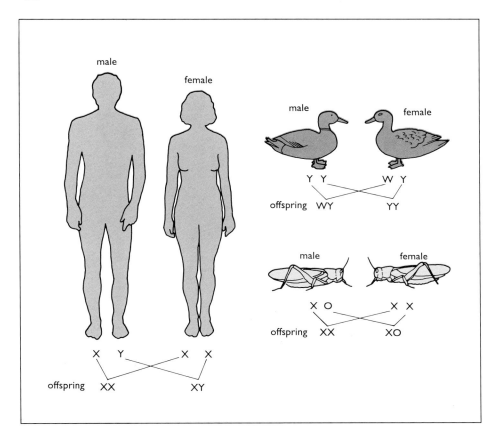

◀ Like all female mammals, women have two X chromosomes in their cells and so all mammal eggs contain a single X chromosome. In males the sex chromosomes are of two different types and so each sperm will contain either an X chromosome or a Y chromosome. When a sperm and an egg meet at the moment of fertilization, a combination of two X chromosomes will produce a male child while a combination of an X and a Y will produce a female child. In birds it is the male cells that contain matching chromosomes, while in many insects the male cells carry only a single chromosome and the sperm receive this or nothing at all. In each case, however, the arrangement produces equal numbers of male and female offspring.

Male-producing sperm and female-producing sperm are very similar, but there are slight differences. For practical purposes, the most important difference is that the female-producing sperm carry a slightly larger version of chromosome number 23. One result is that these female-producing sperm are slightly heavier, and this fact has been used in animal breeding work. Sperm that has been collected from a breeding male can be put into a machine called a centrifuge and spun extremely fast. The slightly heavier female-producing sperm tend to sink to the bottom of the container, so that the two types of sperm are separated. In this way it is possible to obtain a sample of sperm that is highly likely to produce only one sex of offspring. However, the complexity and expense of doing this means that the procedure is not widely used in practice.

Why Are There As Many Males As Females?

One ram can fertilize an entire field full of ewes, and a stallion can cover (mate with) ten mares every day for weeks. There is no need to have as many males as females for sheep or horses to breed successfully. But when the lambs or foals are born, half of them will be male. It seems such a waste of effort to produce all those spare males when far fewer would still keep the population breeding. Natural selection is supposed to eliminate wasted effort, so how has this system evolved?

In the wild, rams fight fiercely during the breeding season, and the ram that wins these fights mates with virtually all the ewes in the flock. Each of these ewes will give birth to one or two lambs. If these are female and survive to breed in their turn, each will have one or two lambs every year. If they are male, they may sire 30 or 40 lambs in a single season, but if they are weaklings and lose their fights they may

▼ In most sporting events men and women compete separately because they have different abilities and strengths. The two sexes complement each other, and in the population as a whole there are almost exactly equal numbers of men and women.

sire none. *On average* the rams are as productive as the ewes. Producing female offspring is safe because they are virtually sure of producing a few lambs. But producing a male is a gamble. He may be a failure, but he may be famously successful. The best strategy is to produce the same number of each sex, which is exactly what the genetic determination of sex achieves.

Of course, if the female could predict which of her male offspring were likely to be failures, and give birth to females instead, then she could exploit the system very effectively. Remarkably, females of some species are able to do just that.

Biologists working in South America have found that among spider monkeys, three-quarters of the young born each year are female. Spider monkeys live in loosely-knit groups. Mothers carry their daughters and nurse them for the first 18 months of their lives. Being bigger, sons require even more care. They are carried for longer, and may still be nursing at two years old, which is a considerable strain on the mother. Producing sons is also a risk for the mother because only the strongest males are likely to succeed in mating when they reach adulthood. Subordinate, low-ranking females are under most pressure. They are weaker, get less food, and are least able to help their sons establish a dominant position in the troop as they mature.

Subordinate females overcome the worst effects of this pressure by not giving birth to sons. It seems that if a male is conceived by a low-ranking female, it simply does not develop and the foetus is reabsorbed. High-ranking females, on the other hand, produce equal numbers of sons and daughters.

▲ Male bighorn sheep in North America celebrate the coming of autumn with ferocious head-butting contests. The stronger, older males win these battles, and the victor's prize is the opportunity to mate with most of the females in the flock. Each year some males are spectacularly successful while others are complete failures, fathering no young at all.

What Sex Is a Young Turtle?

Reptiles have very few friends. Crocodiles and alligators have a reputation for eating people. Snakes, whether venomous or not, terrify more people than any other animal. Only the tortoises and terrapins have ever been popular as pets, but even these harmless creatures could hardly be called cuddly. Most people are afraid of reptiles chiefly because they do not understand them, which is a shame because they are every bit as interesting as birds and mammals, particularly in the way they breed.

Some lizards and snakes give birth to live young, but most reptiles lay eggs. These are very like birds' eggs except that they have soft, leathery shells. The embryo inside an egg grows best if it can be kept at exactly the right temperature. Birds keep their eggs at about 37°C (roughly human body temperature) by warming them with their bodies, or by standing over them to shade them from the sun. If the egg is kept above or below this critical temperature, it will take longer to hatch, and the chick will be weaker.

▲ Newly hatched leathery sea turtles scurry over the sand on their way to the sea. The female laid her eggs in a pit she dug on the beach several months earlier, and the hatchling turtles dig their way to the surface and head for the sea purely by instinct.

Most reptiles cannot keep their eggs warm by sitting on them because they are "cold blooded". Alligators and crocodiles would probably squash them anyway if they tried, so they try to keep them warm in other ways. Tortoises and turtles bury their eggs in warm sand, but alligators (and some crocodiles) build nests of weeds and grasses. These nests are big mounds, with the eggs buried in the middle. As the pile begins to rot, it heats up, in the same way as a garden compost heap or a pile of grass cuttings gets hot after a few days.

A turtle egg buried in the sand on a warm, sunny beach might be at the perfect temperature, but a little deeper, or a little closer to the hot sand at the surface, conditions are very different. Turtle eggs laid too close to the burning surface of the sand soon get cooked, and the embryo inside dies. But deeper down, even quite small differences in temperature have very unexpected results. If the temperature in the nest is below 28°C while the eggs are developing, all the young turtles will be males. If the temperature is above 33°C, all the eggs hatch into females. And if the nest is between 28°C and 33°C, there will be roughly equal numbers of each. In mammals, a baby's sex is decided by the chromosomes that it inherits from its parents, and the same is true in birds and insects. But in crocodiles, alligators, turtles and some lizards, the young animal's sex depends on the temperature of the egg while the embryo inside is growing.

Turtles are peculiar, but it is even more surprising to find that in alligators and crocodiles, temperature has the *opposite* effect. Eggs that are laid in a hot place hatch out male crocodiles and eggs that are laid on cool, shaded river banks, or near the edge of an alligator's compost heap, hatch out females. The role of temperature in deciding the sex of reptiles may even explain the disappearance of the dinosaurs.

Whatever happened to the dinosaurs?

Seventy million years ago the dinosaurs ruled the Earth. Giant beasts like *Triceratops*, with its parrot-like beak and huge horns, and the enormous *Tyrannosaurus*, 16 feet (almost 5m) tall and weighing 8 tons, must once have been fairly common sights in North America. These animals and their relatives lived on Earth for about 140 million years. Some were relatively peaceable animals, feeding on plants, while others, like the famous *Tyrannosaurus*, were fierce predators. Then, quite suddenly, they all died. Rocks 65 million years old still contain fossils of dinosaurs. In rocks more recent than that there are none at all. To this day, no one is really sure exactly what happened.

One idea that might explain the dinosaurs' disappearance is that a massive meteorite, ten miles (16km) across, hit the Earth about 65 million years ago, throwing millions of tons of dust into the air. As the dust swirled around, the skies across the world darkened, and with the dark came changes in the Earth's temperature. Gases released from the rocks by the terrible crash changed the atmosphere into an insulating blanket, heating up the whole world.

Did this sudden and dramatic change in the climate cause the extinction of the dinosaurs? And if

▲ Hadrosaurs laid their eggs on a mound of earth with a slight hollow on top.

so, how? Dinosaurs were reptiles, and so it is possible that, like modern reptiles, the sex of their young was determined by the temperature of their eggs. A change in the air temperature of just a few degrees might have been too much for them. Instead of dinosaur eggs hatching out some males and some females, could it be that for their last few years on the Earth, all dinosaurs were the same sex? It must have been a very miserable end – climate too hot, brain the size of a walnut, and no females.

Or was it no males?

▲ Beautifully preserved hadrosaur nests containing the remains of up to 15 eggs have been found in Montana, USA. These fossils have provided a great deal of new information and show that these dinosaurs took great care of their eggs and often used the same nest-site year after year.

Parental Care

For quite a while, looking after the children is a full-time job, for one parent at least. In fact, humans look after their offspring for longer than any other species of animal, and the amount of care we give them is one of the secrets of our success as a species. Human babies simply cannot survive without the care their parents normally give them, and even older children cannot thrive without the support of their parents.

▲ Teaching them road safety is just one of many ways in which parents keep their children out of danger. Children are unable to concentrate for long, and are easily distracted, so it will be some years before this child can safely cross the road alone.

When a human baby is born, it can do next to nothing for itself. It has to be fed, kept warm, kept dry (but not too dry) and kept clean. It must also be kept safe from animals that might harm it, which might be anything from leopards to the family's pet cat, depending on where the child grows up. All that a baby can do for itself is to cry when it needs something. It is totally dependent on its parents.

As it begins to grow, a small child places even greater demands on its parents. It still needs all the things a baby needs, but as it begins to move around and explore its world it also needs to be kept from harming itself. A very young child learns a lot by experimenting with its world. In particular it tests everything to see if it is good to eat, and for several years one of the parents' many tasks is to try and make sure that this does not include poisonous berries, burning sticks, knives or the cat's tail. During these early years the parents also teach their child a language, which helps them pass on more complicated lessons later in life.

By the time this child reaches maturity and is able to reproduce, its parents will have saved its life thousands of times. They will also have passed on a huge amount of information which will eventually help the child to look after children of its own.

▲ Small children cannot feed themselves. First they must be taught what things are good to eat, and how to eat them. Later they will learn how to prepare food, and how to feed and care for children of their own.

Humans are not the only animals: we simply happen to be the ones we know best, and are most interested in. Not all animals face the same problems as humans in looking after their young: oysters spend very little time worrying about their offspring staying out late! But many animals do care for their young, sometimes for years, and like humans the parents face the problems of keeping their young fed and healthy. They achieve this in a wonderful variety of ways, but each serves the same purpose. Every animal is trying to ensure the survival of its young, and through them the continuation of its family line.

◄ The lioness is a very good mother. She protects her cubs, feeds them and teaches them to hunt. From her they also learn how to take their place in the social hierarchy of the pride.

▲ Mountain gorillas live in compact family groups and look after their infants in very much the same way as humans.

WHY HAVE TWO SEXES?

We are so familiar with animals having two sexes that it is easy to forget to even ask why this should be so. One way of looking at the question is to consider what other possibilities there are.

It is fairly easy to understand why having more than two sexes would be a problem. It is difficult enough to arrange for two animals to get together and cooperate, especially with a complicated mating system such as that of the damselfly. An animal would have serious problems indeed if three or more individuals were required each time it wanted to breed. But that does not answer the question of why, for so many animals, two sexes are so much better than just one. To answer that question we must look at the way animal life has evolved on Earth, and consider the way animals reproduce in the context of the habitats they live in and the various lifestyles they follow.

▶ Damselfly mating is a complex business. The red male holds the female, and then deposits some sperm on his own abdomen. The brown female then arches her body round to collect the sperm.

Like Father Like Son

▼ Cells can divide in two ways. In the example below each cell normally contains four chromosomes. Normal cell division, called mitosis, is shown in the upper part of the diagram. First, each chromosome in the cell is copied exactly. Then, as the cell divides, one of each of the copies goes into one of the new cells so that, like the original cell, each of the daughter cells contains two sets of chromosomes. The lower part of the diagram shows meiosis, a special type of cell division that produces eggs and sperm. As before, the chromosomes are first copied once, but the cell then divides twice so that this time *four* daughter cells are formed – each containing only a single set of chromosomes. In this way, when an egg is fertilized, the single chromosome set from the egg and the single set from the sperm come together to produce a new cell with two sets of chromosomes.

Imagine seeing two friends across a crowded street. Even though there may be hundreds of people walking past, we have no problem in recognizing people we know. We do this by noticing whether they are tall or short, fat or thin, dark or fair. Sometimes we may even recognize them by the way they walk. If they are close enough for us to see their features it is even easier to tell individuals apart, by the colour of their eyes or the shape of the mouth and nose. All people look different until you move in very close indeed.

Look at the same two friends through a microscope and it suddenly becomes very difficult to tell them apart. All people are made up of cells, and the cells of different people all look very much the same. Looking through a microscope it would even be difficult to tell the difference between cells from a person, a parrot and a poodle.

Cells are the basic building blocks of living things. Bricks can be used to build anything from a garage to a skyscraper, and in just the same way, the same types of cells are found in parrots, poodles and people. In all these creatures, muscle cells contract to move arms, legs and wings, nerve cells carry messages to and from the brain, and skin cells form a barrier to keep out dirt and germs.

One important thing about cells is that they are very small, generally too small to be seen without a lens or a microscope. We are all made up of millions of cells (about 60 million in an average adult) and as we grow we must make more of them. To make new cells, an existing one splits in half, and the two new cells can then grow separately.

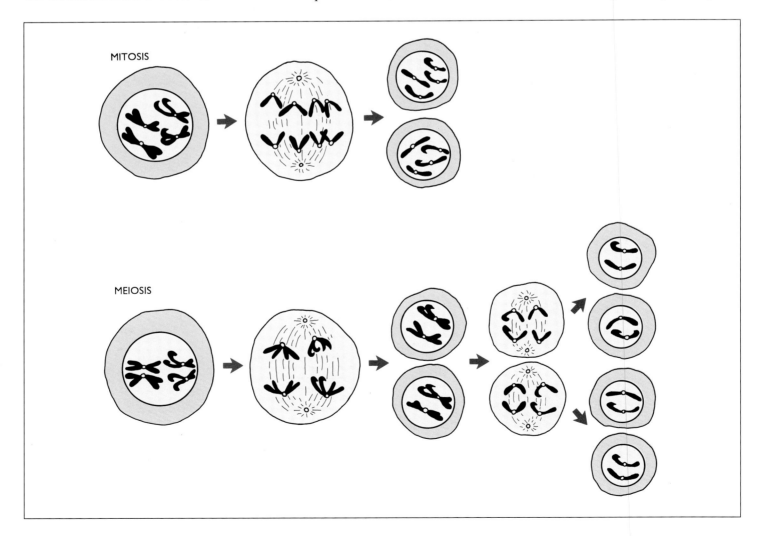

MITOSIS

MEIOSIS

◀ Normally we find it easy to recognize people, but at long range – and especially when dressed in some kind of uniform – it is not so simple. The large numbers worn by these American footballers enable the spectators to indentify individual players.

▼ Under a microscope it is possible to see the individual thread-like chromosomes, especially when the cell is on the point of dividing. With greater magnificaton it is possible to see the coiled structure of the chromatid. What cannot be seen in detail, even with the most powerful microscope, is the molecular structure of the chromatid, shown at the bottom of the diagram. Here the code for life is held in countless combinations of the bases that form the steps of the spiral DNA ladder.

When a cell splits in half, each new cell must have a complete set of instructions if it is to work properly. The part of the cell that carries the instructions is called the nucleus. It is the control centre of the cell, and without it a cell cannot grow or divide. As a cell starts to divide, tiny ribbons appear inside the nucleus. These ribbons are called chromosomes, and it is the chromosomes that carry the instructions that control the cell. The chromosomes make copies of themselves before the cell divides, and each new nucleus gets one copy of each chromosome. The new cells can then grow and divide again, and in this way an animal gets bigger. And because of the way they divide, every cell in an animal's body has an exact copy of the same set of chromosomes.

At first sight it might seem strange for every cell in the body to have the same set of chromosomes. If they all carry the same instructions, how can muscle cells differ from nerve cells? The answer is that muscle and nerve cells do have the same set of instructions, but different *parts* of the chromosomes are active in the different types of cell. These "parts of chromosomes" are called genes, so the genes for making muscle chemicals are active in muscle cells, but not in nerve cells.

We have genes to control the production of millions of chemicals in our bodies. The production of these chemicals keeps our bodies working and it is the slight differences between these chemicals that make us all different from each other. Chemicals even control things like eye colour, hair colour and the way the body grows.

People tend to look rather like their parents, and since it is our genes that determine what we look like, it is a fair guess that we inherit our genes from our parents. This is true, but no one looks *exactly* like either of their parents, because everyone gets half their chromosomes from their father and half from their mother. These half-sets of chromosomes are packaged in special sex cells. The mother's sex cells are her eggs, and the father's are his sperm. With only a half-set of chromosomes each, neither egg nor sperm can grow on its own. But when a sperm joins with an egg, a new complete set of chromosomes is created. This process is called fertilization, and only after this has occurred can a new individual begin its life.

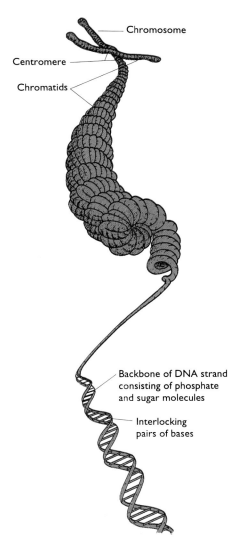

Chromosome

Centromere

Chromatids

Backbone of DNA strand consisting of phosphate and sugar molecules

Interlocking pairs of bases

Eggs and Sperm: Life's "Starter" Pack

Eggs and sperm are different in two important ways. Sperm are small and can move on their own, while eggs are much bigger and unable to move. In fact, in humans and most other animals, the egg is the largest cell in the body and the sperm is the smallest. Sperm and egg each carry a nucleus with chromosomes inside, but the egg is bigger because it carries far more than just its set of chromosomes.

Why are eggs so large and sperm so small? Well, imagine that two people are trying to meet up to go on holiday. If each takes half the luggage, and rushes around town looking for the other, the chances are that they will never meet, and both will end up exhausted. A much more sensible arrangement is for one person to wait at an agreed place and for the other to rush around looking for them. It also makes more sense for the one who is waiting to carry all the luggage.

This is exactly the sort of arrangement that has evolved between eggs and sperm. The egg waits in one place with almost everything that will be needed by the pair when they eventually meet up. The extra baggage that the egg carries is the food it will need after fertilization. The sperm does the rushing around, but all it needs to carry with it is the precious cargo of chromosomes that it is taking to the meeting, plus

The tongue-rolling gene

Some people can stick their tongue out and curve the two edges up so that it makes a hollow tube. This is not a very pretty sight, but it *is* interesting. There is a single gene that decides who can and who cannot do this. The diagram shows how this gene may be passed on through three generations of a typical family. Two of the children cannot roll their tongues, but one can. Their mother cannot roll her tongue (nor can anyone else in her family), so the gene must have come from their father, who got it in turn from his mother.

Not all genes have such obvious effects. Two tall people will probably have tall children, but the children of a tall father and short mother might be almost any size. This is because height is decided by many different genes acting together, and the height of the children depends on exactly which of these genes came from which parent.

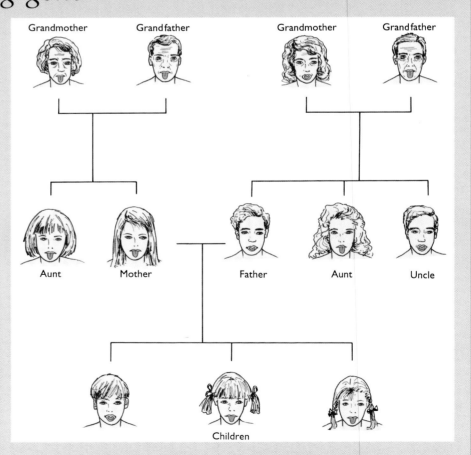

Grandmother   Grandfather   Grandmother   Grandfather

Aunt   Mother   Father   Aunt   Uncle

Children

just enough food to provide it with energy until it gets there. A sperm consists of little more than a nucleus full of chromosomes, and a tail which drives it forward as it swims in search of an egg.

Eggs are packed with food and so it takes a lot of energy for the mother to make them, which means that she cannot produce very many. But there are compensations. Because the egg has so much stored food it can live for quite a long time waiting for a sperm to come along. Sperm on the other hand are tiny. A human male, for example, produces a thousand sperm every second, while a woman releases only about 500 eggs in her entire life. Naturally, only a tiny fraction of the sperm released by a male ever succeed in fertilizing an egg.

▲ A female crab with a batch of eggs attached to the underside of her shell. Like most sea creatures the crab relies on producing huge numbers of eggs in order to ensure that just a few will survive.

Evolution

Every year, a female crocodile lays about 50 eggs. A crab may produce 10,000 eggs. A sea hare can lay an amazing five *million* eggs in a year, and if each of these eggs grew into a sea hare and every female laid another five million eggs, the oceans would soon have no room for anything else. Everything in the sea over-produces, and the only reason why the seas are not crowded with sea hares is that most of the young ones die.

In 1859, Charles Darwin wrote an important book, *On the Origin of Species by Means of Natural Selection*, suggesting that only the young that are best suited to the conditions they find themselves in are likely to live. He described this process as "natural selection". Because only the animals best suited to their environment succeed in breeding, natural selection ensures that only the most efficient animals survive. A crocodile carrying genes that

help it to find more food or swim faster than its rivals will live and have more young. Each generation, more and more crocodiles will carry these useful genes, until eventually almost all crocodiles will have inherited this advantage. Over the centuries, all animals and plants slowly change as natural selection picks out from each generation only those young best adapted to their surroundings. This slow process of change is called evolution.

Fertilization

When a mammal sperm finds an egg, the head of the sperm burrows through the outer coating and into the cell itself. This outer layer is as thin as the surface of a soap bubble, and nothing like the shell of a hen's egg. (Once a hen's egg has been laid it is in no state to be fertilized. A cockerel's sperm would need a drill attached to its head to get through the shell. Birds' eggs have to be fertilized *before* the shell grows round them.)

The first sperm to reach an egg penetrates the outer layer, and almost at once the surface of the egg changes so that no other sperm can get inside. Once the head of the sperm is inside the egg, the chromosomes from the egg and the sperm come together to produce the nucleus of the new individual, and the process of fertilization is completed. Fertilization happens like this in all animals, but different animals have evolved many different ways of getting the egg and sperm together in the first place. How this is done depends very much on the animal, the way it lives, and where it lives.

Eggs and sperm die if they dry out, so fertilization is easiest for animals that live in water. For example, oysters simply release their eggs and sperm into the water. Oysters live alone, attached to rocks at the bottom of the sea, and so this is really the only way that they can get their eggs and sperm together. But the sea is enormous, and the chances that a sperm will just happen to bump into an egg are very low. To improve the chances of their eggs and sperm meeting, even the simplest creatures have evolved some clever tricks. More advanced animals help their sperm fertilize eggs by mating, but mating puts such demands on animals that they have evolved wonderful colours and amazing behaviours to bring it about.

▶▶ This remarkable photograph was taken with a scanning electron microscope and then coloured with the aid of a special computer programme. It shows human sperm beginning to burrow into the outer layer of an egg. Electron microscopes can produce images of objects far too small to be seen with even the most powerful optical microscopes.

Fertilization in plants

Sex in plants is essentially the same as sex in animals. Brown seaweeds like the familiar oarweed, kelp and bladderwrack release eggs and free-swimming sperm into the sea in exactly the same way as oysters. Mosses and liverworts also release free-swimming sperm, but because the sperm will die if they dry out, and because they need water to swim through, these plants can live only in damp places. To invade dry land, plants have had to find ways to get their sperm and eggs together without the sperm drying out. To solve this problem conifers and flowering plants have wrapped the tiny sperm in a water-tight package — the pollen grain.

Once pollen is transferred from the male to the female part of a plant, either blown by the wind or

▲ Bladder wrack is one of the common seaweeds of rocky shorelines.

carried by an animal, the pollen grain grows a long tube which tunnels through the female tissues until it reaches the egg. Here the pollen tube opens to release two sperm cells, each of which will fuse with the nucleus of the egg to begin the development of a new

plant. Because the pollen tube releases the sperm cells so close to the egg, the sperm need no tails. Only in primitive land plants like the Chinese ginkgo tree and the tree-ferns or cycads do the sperm from pollen grains retain a tail. It is a reminder of their origins.

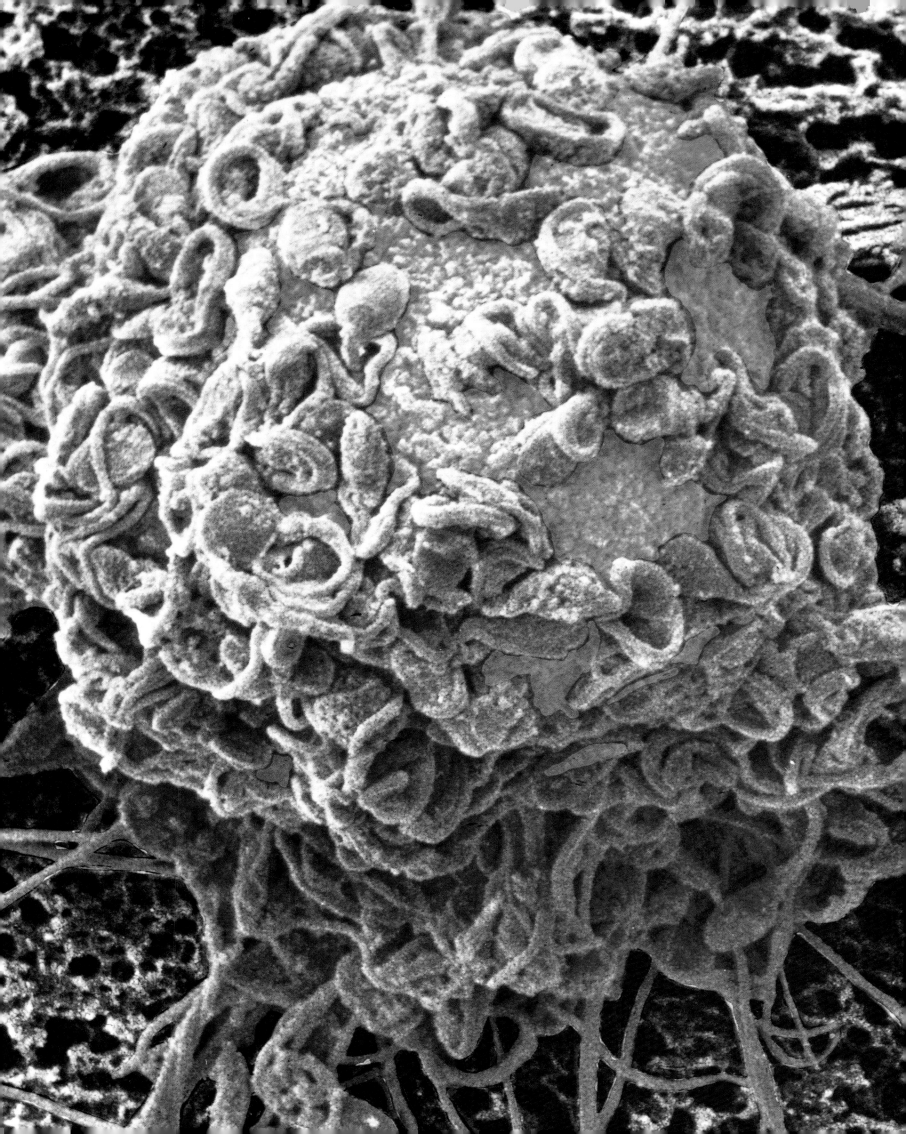

Pairing and Mating

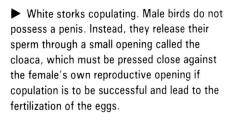

▶ White storks copulating. Male birds do not possess a penis. Instead, they release their sperm through a small opening called the cloaca, which must be pressed close against the female's own reproductive opening if copulation is to be successful and lead to the fertilization of the eggs.

For an animal to breed sexually, the egg and sperm must get together. They can do this if they are simply released into water, but if the parents get together first, the whole job is made much easier. The sperm do not have to swim so far, and they do not have to search such a big area looking for the right eggs.

All sorts of animals pair up before releasing their eggs and sperm. Some starfishes pair up to spawn, and in many fishes the male wraps himself around the female in the water and presses his vent against hers so that the eggs and sperm are as close together as possible when they are released. Male frogs and toads do much the same, the male

gripping the female from behind and waiting until she releases her eggs before releasing his sperm to fertilize them.

Pairing was a terrific evolutionary breakthrough because it greatly increased the chances of sperm finding eggs and fertilizing them successfully. Pairing also allows the fertilized eggs to be put in a safe place. Atlantic salmon live in the sea off Greenland, but before they pair up to breed they swim thousands of miles, making their way to the headwaters of the rivers where they themselves hatched. Here the female digs a shallow hole in the gravel, and as she lays her eggs her partner swims alongside and fertilizes them. Then she covers the eggs

▲ Bush crickets wrap up their sperm in neat packages called spermatophores. The distant ancestors of crickets probably originally passed sperm from male to female by depositing such packages on the ground, much as scorpions and certain other animals do today.

with more gravel, hiding them from the fishes and other creatures that would eat them if they could.

Pairing increases the chances of the sperm meeting the eggs, and the closer the parents get together, the better. This is why many animals do not release unfertilized eggs at all: instead they mate. When animals mate, the eggs stay inside the mother, and the father releases his sperm inside her too. Then the chances of sperm finding egg are really good, and the embryo starts life in a very safe place. Mating results in what is known as internal fertilization, because the egg is fertilized inside the body of the mother.

Sperm must swim through water to reach an egg, and they die very quickly if they dry out. This was an enormous problem for animals when they first started to live on land, and almost all of them solved it by evolving some sort of mating and internal fertilization. With internal fertilization it is possible for the sperm to swim to the egg through a thin film of liquid inside the mother's body. Reptiles, birds, mammals and insects have all evolved internal fertilization, and so − unlike frogs for example − they do not have to go back to the water to breed.

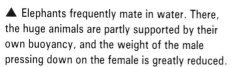

▲ Elephants frequently mate in water. There, the huge animals are partly supported by their own buoyancy, and the weight of the male pressing down on the female is greatly reduced.

Another important advantage of pairing or mating is that it allows the parents to *choose* their partners. This is particularly important for females because they cannot produce many eggs. By making sure that their few eggs are fertilized by the fittest and healthiest males, they improve the chances of their young ones growing up fit and strong enough to raise a family of their own. Males can produce so many sperm that they can fertilize many females, so they do not need to be so choosy. However, by pairing up with a female who is just about to lay, they can try to make sure that it is their sperm and not those of some other male that fertilize her eggs.

◄ Many fish rub up against each other during courtship, as a preparation for mating. In many species, males and females wrap their bodies around each other so that their eggs and sperm are released into the water as close together as possible, which greatly increases the chances of fertilization.

The Importance of Timing

▶ Elephant seals all come ashore at the same time in order to breed. The pregnant females give birth to their young, and then mate again before returning to the sea. There is nothing gentle or cooperative about mating in this species. The aggressive bulls attempt to mate with as many females as possible, and during the few brief weeks ashore, many females and up to one in ten of the new-born pups may be crushed by the massive rampaging bull seals.

Most animals are unable to breed all the year round because reproduction takes a lot of energy. It takes energy to find a mate and to help the fertilized eggs survive. It takes energy even to make eggs and sperm. But if animals do not make the effort to reproduce, they become extinct. What animals have to do is reproduce efficiently and not waste their efforts. The more efficiently an animal can reproduce itself, the more offspring it will leave behind. One way to improve efficiency is to time things so that male and female are both ready to breed at the same time, and so that the young are born when there is plenty of food for them to eat.

Food is usually much easier to find in summer, when the warmth of the Sun brings out a lush new growth of greenery. Deer have their fawns in spring, so while the doe is feeding herself and also making milk for her young, there is a rich supply of fresh, nutritious grass and young herbs and shrubs for her to eat. Most woodland birds nest in spring, taking advantage of the glut of caterpillars that feast on the fresh young tree leaves. Emperor penguins lay their eggs in the middle of the Antarctic winter, which is not as crazy as it sounds because the young can only survive if they fledge in the brief Antarctic summer when there is plenty of food in the sea.

Breeding seasons are timed so that the young have the best chance of survival, but survival does not depend only on finding enough food. Young animals are particularly vulnerable to predators. Many must learn from their parents the sights and smells that warn of danger, but even so the young are usually slow to escape. Giving birth to all the young in a single short season improves the chances that at least some will survive. On the African plains, young wildebeest fall prey to lions and hyenas, and the mother can do little to defend her calf. Nevertheless, the chances of any individual surviving are good, because wildebeest herds are huge and all the young in a herd are born at the same time. During the period when the young are most vulnerable, the predators simply have more food available than they can possibly eat. Young born early or late would emerge into a world full of hungry predators.

In South America, all the females in a troop of squirrel monkeys give birth within days of each other. Usually there are no more than 20 or 30 squirrel monkeys in each troop, and the few young they raise each year are hardly enough to satisfy all the predators in the area. In this case the advantage of having all the young born at the same time is that during the first few weeks, when the young monkeys are particularly at risk, the whole troop can concentrate on looking out for predators. Ornate hawk-eagles and forest falcons are particularly dangerous, swooping down to pick off any unguarded youngster, but with alert eyes scanning the sky throughout the day, the monkeys usually get enough warning to scuttle to safety.

Mayflies and cicadas: how to avoid predators

By gathering together in larger groups to mate, many animals expose themselves to the risk of being eaten. During the first week of June every year, one such gathering drives trout and trout-fishermen crazy. The trout start feeding like mad, the fishermen spend every minute of the day trying to catch them, and it is all because of an insect called the mayfly.

Mayflies spend one or two years living as nymphs in the gravel at the bottom of the river, and during this one week in June the adults emerge. They fly weakly from the water surface to the nearby bushes, where they moult. Next evening the males dance in great swarms near the river, and as a female flies through the swarm she is grasped and mated by one of the males. Within hours the female has laid her eggs and is dead. Within a week not a single mayfly can be found.

Mayflies pose two questions. Why are they called mayflies when they come out in June, and why do they all emerge at the same time? Until 1731, mayflies did indeed emerge in May, and it is because they appeared so predictably at this time of year that they got their name. But in 1732, the British Government altered the calendar, taking 11 days out of the year and pushing the last bit of May, and the mayflies, into June.

It is more difficult to understand why all the mayflies emerge at the same time. Visit a trout stream when the mayflies are out and this mass emergence looks like mass suicide. It is not only the trout that gorge themselves on the mayflies;

▲ An adult American periodical cicada makes its first appearance after 17 years underground.

every bird for miles around joins in the feast. Even blackbirds which usually take worms, and sparrows, which normally eat seeds, flit about catching the weak-flying insects. Tens of thousands are eaten, but because hundreds of thousands emerge in each hatching, most of them survive. If they emerged to breed throughout the summer, say ten thousand a week, the predators would be able to take virtually all of them. As it is, the predators eat all they can, but once they are full they quickly lose interest. The best time for any one mayfly to emerge is when all the others are emerging. That way it will have a reasonable chance of survival — and of finding a mate.

The periodical cicadas of North America have taken this predator-swamping tactic a step further. There are several species of periodical cicada, and they have what is probably the strangest life-cycle of any insect. No adults are seen for many years, and then quite suddenly millions emerge. For two weeks no one in the area gets an afternoon nap because the calls of even a few thousand cicadas are deafening. During this brief spell the adults mate, lay their eggs on the woody stems of trees and bushes, and then die. The eggs hatch, the nymphs fall to the ground and burrow into the soil, and below ground a new generation of larvae begins its slow development. Depending on the species, this may take 13 or 17 years, after which the adult insects emerge and the cycle is repeated. How they measure the passing of time is a mystery, but their lifestyle means that no predator can possibly survive by living on periodical cicadas alone!

▲ The greatest time of danger for a wildebeest is during the first few hours of life, when the new-born animal is weak and barely able to stand.

▲ The new-born calf must quickly find its feet if it is to have any chance of avoiding predators and keeping up with the migrating herd.

◀ Female wildebeest all give birth at the same time because they mate only during a brief period when the Moon is full. In a single herd there may be several thousand animals, yet most of the calves are born within a few days of each other. While they are young and helpless they are easy prey for lions and cheetahs. Even so, most will survive because with so many born at the same time there is a limit to the number the predators can eat.

◀ For the young that do survive the hazards of the first few days there are still dangers ahead during the long migration across the plains and rivers of East Africa, but as their legs grow stronger and their stamina increases they are soon able to stay close to their mothers and find protection within the mass of animals forming the herd.

Animal Clocks

How can animals know the right time to start breeding? Some have little choice but to wait until conditions are right. Spadefoot toads, for example, spend the winter buried deep beneath the sands of the Sonoran Desert and have no way of knowing the seasons. They must wait until the first rains of summer penetrate their burrows before venturing out to breed in ponds and puddles. In the dark depths of the oceans, starfish wait until a steady rain of debris from above signals that summer has begun and that at the surface the Sun is once again encouraging a bloom of plankton growth. But most animals will breed more successfully if they can predict exactly when conditions will be right, and prepare themselves in advance: they need a clock.

For a clock to be any use, it must keep accurate time, and it must tell the time in the right-sized units. In other words it is no use having only a second hand on a watch if what you really need to know is the date, or the hour. There are several natural clocks that have these qualities, and animals use them to time their breeding seasons.

The Sun is one such clock, and it can be used by animals as it is by people to tell the time of day. The capercaillie, like many birds, mates only in the early morning and takes its cue from the rising Sun. But the Sun can also tell animals the time of year. As summer approaches, the days get longer and many animals start to come into breeding condition in response to this signal. Wading birds migrate to their breeding areas, male chaffinches start to sing and fight for territory, and European toads head off to their traditional breeding ponds. Deep in a murky pond, it may not be so obvious that the days are getting longer, but as the Sun gets higher in the sky and the cold nights get shorter, the temperature of the water rises steadily. Many fishes rely on this indirect clock to tell them that it is time to change into their spring courtship colours and begin breeding.

▼ In order to mate successfully, sockeye salmon must find their way back from the sea to the stream of their birth – an astonishing feat of navigation – and they must also arrive at exactly the right time.

Not all animals breed in spring. For some creatures the shortening days of autumn mark the beginning of the breeding season. Crossbills are finches that feed on pine cones. Their food supply is at its best during winter — and that is when they breed.

The Sun is a useful clock for measuring both the days and the seasons, but because very few animals can count up to 30, it is not much use for measuring months. And yet, like humans, many animals find the month to be a useful measure of time. Sea creatures in particular often breed at monthly intervals. They are guided not by the Sun, but by the phases of the Moon. Every 28 days, when the Moon is full, the sky is lit by moonlight. As the Moon wanes, a thinner and thinner crescent reflects less of the Sun's rays and the nights grow darker, until at the new Moon there is no moonlight at all. At the same time, the changing phases of the Moon affect the tides, new and full Moons producing the extra-large "spring" tides. Many animals can detect these changes and use them to time their breeding, each responding to the clock in different ways. Sea urchins spawn at full Moon, oysters spawn both at full Moon and new Moon, and certain seaweeds only spawn at the half-Moon. Fish like the grunion, which breed only at the highest tides of the month, must be especially attuned to the changes in the Moon's cycle.

Even wildebeest on the African plains, miles from the nearest ocean, use the Moon as a clock. Once the grass begins to grow in spring, signalling the start of the breeding season, most wildebeest wait until the full Moon before they mate. In this way they make sure that most of the calves will be born at exactly the same time, a neat bit of "fine tuning" which helps to outwit the predators by ensuring that there are far more young wildebeest than the hunters can possibly kill.

▲ Grunion mate and lay their eggs in the sand at high tide when the Moon is full and the tide reaches its highest point on the beach. Their eggs will remain safe under the sand until the next New Moon when the tide will again be at its highest level.

Why Is Sex Such a Good Idea?

It is not immediately obvious why sexual reproduction is a good thing. Certainly reproduction is essential, but sexual reproduction is a very complicated business. It is also dangerous and takes up a great deal of an animal's time and energy. Animals will not survive for long if they take unnecessary risks, or waste time and energy, so there must be an enormous advantage to sexual reproduction. But what is it?

▲ The deadly charge of this hunting lioness shows one of the advantages of sexual reproduction. In each generation of a species, some animals will be faster than average, others a little slower. Some may be tall, some short. Some may be resistant to diseases that wipe out their brothers and sisters, while some may have colouring that provides them with good protection. Those that inherit useful characteristics – like the speed and power of the lioness – will survive and pass them on to the next generation. Those that do not will die.

The question poses quite a problem, for there are many animals (and plants for that matter) that reproduce on their own, without sex. Some of these animals produce hundreds or even thousands of offspring just by repeatedly splitting in half. They never trouble with the complicated business of courtship and sex at all. But there is a difference between offspring produced sexually and those produced without sex, and this difference involves the cells and chromosomes of the animals.

Most of the animals that reproduce without sex are unfamiliar little blobs of life that are either too small to see or live in ponds or on the sea bed. To find familiar living things that can reproduce without sex we must look to the world of plants. Strawberry plants put out long "runners" and at the end of each of these a new plant will grow. Because the new plant contains *exactly* the same chromosomes as the old one, it will be an exact copy – the same colour of flowers, the same scent, and the same resistance (or vulnerability) to diseases.

Raise a new generation of strawberry plants from seed, however, and the outcome is very different. No two plants will be quite the same, and the reason is that strawberry plants can reproduce both asexually (without sex) and sexually – and seeds are the result of *sexual* reproduction. When each seed is formed, half its chromosomes come from each parent and they are mixed together to produce the new individual. None of the seedlings is ever quite like the "mother" plant, or quite like the plant that provided the pollen. Nor are any two seedlings quite like each other.

Plants and animals that reproduce sexually end up producing a range of different offspring and these are likely to be suited to a range of different conditions. Some of them may be better suited than either of their parents were to the conditions in which they live. Some may be able to survive even when conditions change. This is the big advantage of sexual reproduction. Sex produces variety, and variety is more than the spice of life, it is an essential ingredient – the key to survival and success.

Without sex, animals and plants can only go on producing endless identical copies of themselves. Only if there are mistakes in the copying process can they produce anything new. Sex allows different genes to be shuffled together every time, so that every individual animal is a sort of living experiment in how well any particular combination of genes works. Many combinations of genes are failures, and the individuals carrying them fail to breed either because they cannot find a mate or because they cannot escape their enemies. On the other hand, successful combinations may allow an animal to take over a new habitat, or even begin the process of evolution into a completely new species. This is the advantage of sexual reproduction, and the fact that so many creatures use sex proves just how much that advantage outweighs the problems.

▲ This fossilized crayfish lived millions of years ago. It is not quite the same as its modern descendants because crayfish, like all animals, have evolved in that time. However, its very close similarity to modern crayfish shows what a good and successful basic design this is for an aquatic creature.

FINDING A MATE

Bookshops are full of stories that start with "boy meets girl" because for humans finding a member of the opposite sex is very easy. We meet each other at school, at work, at discos and at parties. The problem for humans is not finding a member of the opposite sex: it is finding the right one. But for many species the problem is often one of finding a member of the same species but opposite sex in the first place.

For an animal the size of a beetle, the chances of just happening to bump into a suitable partner are very small. It cannot travel very fast, or very far, and the world is a very big place. Finding a mate by sight alone would be like looking for a needle in a haystack. Animals may solve this problem by using other senses such as smell and hearing, whose power we humans cannot even imagine. Some animals also use a strategy rather like going to a party — but some of these methods mean the animal taking enormous risks.

▶ Girls admiring athletes at the Prague Spartakiad in 1985. Although visual attraction is important, it is only one of many factors that are involved when humans set about choosing a partner.

Sounds Attractive

▶ Mole crickets "sing" from the safety of their burrows by scratching a toothed scraper on one wing against a "file" on the other – rather like running a finger-nail along the teeth of a comb. The funnel-like shape of the burrow amplifies the sound, which can be heard up to half a mile (0.8km) away.

Birds sing, frogs croak and grasshoppers scratch, all for the same reason – to attract a mate. Making sounds is one of the best ways to attract attention because sound travels round corners. This, of course, is why you can hear the telephone ring in the next room. Sound is made when something vibrates. The bell inside a telephone rings because it is hit by a small hammer which sets it vibrating. The vibrations move the air around the bell, and like other animals we hear the sound because our ears can sense these movements in the air.

Animals have many different ways of making noises, but they all involve making something vibrate. Male mosquitos home in on the high-pitched whine of a female's beating wings, and male deathwatch beetles communicate by banging their bodies against the wooden walls of their tunnels. Sounds also travel well through water, and fish can make noises by vibrating their swim bladders, grinding their teeth or by literally rubbing their bones together. Without doubt though, the greatest underwater singers of all are the whales, and like all mammals they have specialized sound-producing organs in their throats. This allows them to make an enormous range of noises, and like birds and frogs, whales sing to attract females. However, one big problem with making sound in order to communicate is that if one animal can hear the sound, others can hear it as well, and that will often include predators as well as potential mates.

On land, birds and mammals can get round this problem of attracting the wrong sort of attention by using different types of sound. Predatory birds and mammals find it hard to pinpoint a singer if it calls repeatedly on the same note, with no sudden starts or stops. Songs like this are used by animals that wish to announce their presence without giving away their exact position. Small flocking birds often make these "contact calls" while feeding, and these calls help to keep the flock together to the benefit of all its members.

Songs with a wide range of notes and sharp changes in volume are particularly useful for attracting a mate because they are very distinctive and easier to locate. But of course these songs also reveal the singer to its predators. A male nightingale has to run this risk if he is to attract a mate, so he plays a risky game of "hide and sing". His song makes it easy to work out where he is sitting, but by singing from the middle of a thicket he is pretty safe from attack, and from there he can keep a careful look-out for foxes and hawks.

The farther a sound travels, the more chance there is that it will attract a mate, so animals have developed a number of tricks to make their calls louder and to make them carry farther. Humans use similar tricks to make their musical instruments sound louder. Most stringed instruments, for example, have a sound-box which amplifies the sound of the string, and frogs have something very similar. They make their own sound-boxes by blowing up a great balloon of skin beneath the chin or at either side of the throat. Crickets make their chirping calls by rubbing their wing covers together. Even without amplification these calls can sometimes be heard from over half a mile (0.8km) away, but a cricket can do even better than that by using the mouth of its burrow as a sound-box. Mole crickets have refined this technique, and the mouths of their burrows are built like miniature antique gramophone horns to increase their sound output.

Only recently it has been discovered that elephants have a very different way of making their calls travel farther. As well as their familiar trumpeting, elephants can make a deep rumbling sound, so low in pitch that human ears cannot hear it. These deep sounds can travel incredible distances. Using special microphones, researchers have found that male elephants make these low-frequency sounds when searching for receptive females, and the females must be able to hear the sounds because they answer them from many miles away.

▲ The male spiny reed frog has an inflatable pouch of skin on his throat which acts as a sound-box and makes his calls sound much louder.

The Sweet Smell of Success

Bagworms are unusual little moths. They take their odd name from the habit of their larvae, which make little bags for themselves from silk, bits of bark, pieces of leaf and grains of sand. The bagworms spend their lives hauling these protective mobile homes around the trees in which they live, and when the time comes for them to pupate they fix the bag firmly to a leaf or twig and remain inside.

The adults that emerge from the pupae are rather dull in colour, but what they lack in beauty they make up for in interest. The females of most species of bagworm have no wings, and never leave their protective bags. Instead, they simply release a scent. Special receptors on the male's antennae are unbelievably sensitive to this smell and can detect a female from many miles away. The male flies toward the source of the smell, and mates with the female by slipping his abdomen inside her silken sac. Once fertilized, the female lays between 500 and 1,000 eggs inside the bag, and then she dies.

▶ Female vapourer moths, like female bagworms, have no wings. They are unable to go out and search for a mate themselves, so they attract their partners by releasing a distinctive scent known as a pheromone.

The story of the bagworm moth tells us a lot about animals that use smell to find their mates. When females waft a distinctive and very personal scent into the air, males can become incredibly sensitive to it. There is no other way that such a small animal could attract a mate from such a great distance. And being such a distinctive scent, it can be difficult or impossible for other animals to detect it. This is an important difference between smell and hearing. A frog's croak is not directed at us, but we can hear it, and so can most other animals. By homing in on the sound, night hunters can find frogs and eat them – hardly the sort of attention the frogs set out to attract by their croaking. By contrast there are no predators that can smell out the female bagworm as she produces her scent.

There are other advantages in using smell to attract a mate. Animals that leave a lingering scent do not have to stay in the same place and wait for a mate to arrive. Many female snakes produce a scent when they are in breeding condition. As they slither along, they leave behind them a scent trail for passing males to pick up. In much the same way male rhinoceroses kick through piles of their own dung to make sure their footsteps can easily be followed by passing females.

Animals use scents to do much more than just attract a mate. Mammals like cheetahs produce a scent in their urine that signals when they are in breeding condition, but scents in the urine of social animals (those that live in groups) often provide even more information. A male wolf that leaves a scent-mark is telling other animals about his sex, his breeding condition, and his position in the social hierarchy. Domestic dogs do much the same thing, producing a complicated world of scent communication that is still something of a mystery to humans. Bear in mind that a dog's sense of smell is fifty times more sensitive than ours: to the dog, scent is far more important than sight – especially at long range.

▲ Scent marks can be used to leave messages that remain long after the animal that made them has left the area. Here, a tigress sniffs at a tree that was sprayed with scent by a male several days earlier. The tiger's scent mark warns other males that they are trespassing on his territory. It tells the tigress that she is in the territory of a mature male – a potential mate.

Flowers, Fence-posts and Hilltops

It may sound odd, but not many animals find their mates by looking for them. To find a mate by looking for her, a male must be in exactly the right place at exactly the right time, and even then he might easily miss seeing her if she is camouflaged or happens to be behind a tree.

Animals that use their eyes to find their mates generally live where there is little chance of anything getting in the way. Deep sea fishes flash luminous signals to each other through the empty vastness of the oceans. Zebra spiders living on flat walls and bare rock faces rely on their eyes both to hunt their prey and to search for their partners. But more often, animals use their eyes to find a place where they will meet their mates, rather than to find them directly.

Males have a better chance of meeting a mate if they wait in a place that females will be drawn to. Male bees of many species seek out clumps of flowers and wait close by for females arriving in search of food. Some male hummingbirds use the same trick, staking their claim to a patch of nectar-rich flowers and allowing females to feed there only if they accept the male as a mate.

▼ Zebra spiders use their huge eyes to search for their mates. These enormous, forward-facing eyes are unlike those of most other spiders. They can be moved up and down, and from side to side, and they can also be focused by shifting them backwards and forwards. They can even be rotated slightly, a movement that is used to pin-point prey — or a mate.

Food supplies are easy to control when they are scarce, but when food is plentiful females can easily feed without ever going near a male. In this case, any obvious landmark can become a meeting place. Such landmarks must be prominent, and both sexes must recognize them as meeting and mating places. These landmarks often have nothing to do with the animals' day-to-day lives. In the deserts of Arizona, male hairstreak butterflies spend their days patrolling hilltops, where sooner or later the females will come to mate. There, they also meet tarantula hawk wasps that use the same landmarks as mating places. In the same deserts, harvester ants use any vertical posts as meeting places. The day after the first heavy rains of summer, swarms of male ants dance above the most prominent fence-posts, waiting impatiently for females to arrive. Before the ranchers arrived and covered the land with fence-posts, the ants probably met over dead tree stumps or anything else that stood up from the ground.

▼ This night photograph shows the dancing trails of courting fireflies. The insects produce the light chemically, and the rhythm of the males' flashes attracts females of the right species. However, using lights does involve a risk as they may also attract predators.

By using such landmarks as meeting places these creatures may be avoiding one of the most serious problems for animals that find their mates by sight. If a male makes a sound to advertise himself, he can be heard even when he cannot be seen. This makes it more likely that he will be found by his mate and reduces the danger that he will be found by his enemies. In the same way, animals that use scent to attract their mates can hide themselves from predators. Animals that attract attention visually cannot hide at the same time. They run the greatest risk of being eaten and so must use every trick they can in order to survive the hazards of the breeding season.

The Risks
of
Advertising

Whenever an animal advertises for a mate, it is taking a risk. The risk is that it will be found by the wrong animal – a predator or a parasite rather than a mate. Calling mud-puddle frogs are eaten by bats. Calling crickets are attacked by parasitic flies. Displaying mayflies are eaten by birds. A bark beetle attracts its mate by scent, but there is a predatory beetle that can also follow the trail. Whichever way an animal advertises, there is a danger that it could also be attracting its own killer.

It is usually the males that take the risk of advertising, not because male animals are particularly brave (or stupid) but because of the fundamental difference between males and females. A male produces billions of sperm, so the more often he can mate, the more eggs he can fertilize. A female on the other hand produces a small number of much larger eggs, and she may only need to mate once to fertilize all of them. Extra matings will not help her: on the contrary, they will just make her life more dangerous.

Advertising is risky, but for males the risk is worthwhile because there is a chance that they will be able to mate many times and father lots of offspring. For females it is hardly ever worth the risk of advertising for a mate. The female's precious eggs are her only chance of passing on her genes to the next generation, and a male is almost

certain to find her even if she does nothing. In their different ways, each individual male and female produces as many of its own young as possible, and this is the basis of evolutionary success.

Like all the best rules, this one has its exceptions. Although females rarely advertise their presence by singing or dancing, the bagworm moth is one that uses scent to attract males. But in this case the exception really does prove the rule. The female bagworm, tucked away in her silken shroud, is safe. No predators can home in on her subtle scent, and it is the male bagworm moths that take the real risk by flying in search of the females. As they fly to the female, they expose themselves to predators, and perhaps even more importantly, males can actually be deceived by their predators and lured to their death.

Bolas spiders use an unusual technique for hunting their prey. Instead of constructing a normal web they hang upside-down from a twig and dangle a single, sticky thread. The spiders then release a barrage of smells that mimic the scents released by the females of several different species of moth. Male moths flying in to investigate the scents become trapped in the sticky thread and are grabbed and eaten by the spiders. It is just one of the many kinds of mimicry found in the animal world – with the predator this time copying the mating scent of the female of its prey species.

▲ Most bats locate their prey by producing high-frequency sound which operates very like radar. As the sound strikes an object, some is reflected back, and the bat uses the reflected signals to home in on its prey. The frog-eating bat of Central America uses a rather different technique. Instead of using the echoes of its own voice, it homes in on the croaks of mud-puddle frogs as they call to attract a mate.

COURTSHIP

If an animal appears to be doing something totally ridiculous, it is probably courting. Birds of paradise almost turn themselves inside-out as part of their courtship displays. Newts solemnly dance across the mud at the bottom of their ponds. Some fish swim standing on their heads. Courtship must be important if it can turn the animal world upside-down in this way.

Courtship is a matter of choosing the right partner, or of one animal persuading another that the two of them would make perfect partners. The really strange thing is that turning yourself inside-out, dancing in mud or standing on your head should help to do this. The whole business of animal courtship is very strange, fascinating, and often very beautiful.

▶ Like many mammals, harvest mice use their sense of smell as a means of communication. Here, a pair of mice sniff each other during courtship.

Getting in Close

Courtship is not the same thing as finding a mate. A peacock does not put up his magnificent fan-shaped tail in order to find a peahen: he does it standing right in front of one. The male has to go through his performance before the female will mate with him. These courtship displays are often very beautiful, which is why for centuries rich people have kept peacocks and mandarin ducks in their gardens. To animals, courtship displays are not works of art but important rituals packed with information. A displaying male peacock is telling a female about his species, sex, health and status – information that will help her to decide whether or not to mate with him.

To advertise for mates, animals must use signals that travel long distances, but courtship signals are used at close range and therefore they can be more subtle. A male cricket makes a very loud noise to attract females, but when one approaches, he changes his tune. His courtship song is a much softer call, less likely to attract the attention of predators. Junglefowl are the ancestors of the domestic chicken, and males attract females by crowing like farmyard cockerels. But whether or not a female mates with a particular male depends not on his voice but on the size of his comb and the colour of his eyes.

▲ In humans, courtship often starts from simple attraction. We see someone whose looks we like, start up a conversation, and then slowly start to get to know each other.

▶ Black-headed gulls use their dark heads in their threat displays, so during courtship they adopt a submissive posture or turn the head and body away to avoid any risk of signalling aggression.

Because courtship signals are exchanged at close quarters, the senses of sight and touch become particularly important. These senses would be useless, or even dangerous, if used for attracting a mate at long range, but are perfect for exchanging information at short range without attracting attention. Blister beetles are just one example of an insect whose courtship involves touch, with the male repeatedly stroking and grasping the female's antennae. The touch of a male is important in releasing the sexual responses of many female mammals, and many female fishes too.

Perhaps the most subtle form of courtship communication yet discovered is that used by the green knife-fish. Knife-fishes are relatives of the electric eel. They live in the lakes of Venezuela, and like electric eels they have a special organ capable of generating a small electric current. Unlike the eels though, the knife-fishes do not use these electric shocks for stunning their prey. Instead they are used in courtship, and the male courts the female by changing the pattern of discharges from his electric organ. Such secret signals are understood by the female but are unlikely to attract the unwelcome attention of a predator, since none of the local predator species are equipped to "tune in" to this highly specialized "language".

▲ Mating is a dangerous game for venomous animals such as these Saharan yellow scorpions. During courtship they grasp each other's pincers, and keep well clear of the deadly tail stings.

How the mandarin got his fan

Rudyard Kipling's stories for children tell how the leopard got his spots by changing his skin, and how the camel got his hump as a punishment for not doing his share of the work. The *Just-So Stories* say nothing about ducks, but the true story of how the mandarin got his fan shows that evolutionary fact can be almost as strange as fiction.

According to the theory of evolution, all ducks once looked much the same. As they spread out across the world, some came to live on great lakes, others on fast-flowing rivers, yet others on shallow ponds. Time passed, and natural selection changed these ducks so that each became adapted to its new home. As these different ducks became more specialized, it became more and more important for them to make sure they mated only with others of their own kind. A hybrid between a river duck and a lake duck would probably not be able to swim against a fast current *or* dive to the bottom cf a deep lake.

Female ducks unable to tell the difference between their own kind and others would have raised many of these hybrids, all unable to compete for food with the specialized lake and river birds. Today such hybrids are rare in nature. Evolution has selected those ducks that can recognize their own kind, and has selected drakes that are best at advertising the differences between themselves and other species. Anything that distinguishes one species from another may be used by females to identify their own kind.

Different types of duck use different techniques for getting their food, so it is hardly surprising that several species use their feeding techniques as a means of identification. Shovelers, for example, skim their food from the surface of the water, and this

▲ The magnificent colours and unique courtship behaviour of the mandarin drake leave females in no doubt about which species he belongs to.

distinctive behaviour has been incorporated into the "mock feeding" display that precedes mating. The courtship display no longer involves actual feeding — it has become a ritual in which the distinctive actions of feeding have been stylized and exaggerated as a way of identifying the birds to each other.

Most birds seem to become rather uncomfortable and nervous during courtship, and it is often possible to see that they are torn between their desire to move together and mate, and their fear of each other. In many birds, the male and female turn their heads away from each other during courtship, signalling that they do not intend to use their bills as weapons. A drake trying to mate must approach a female, but he also wants to avoid the fight that would normally result from moving too close to another adult animal. In similar uncomfortable circumstances, humans might pick bits of cotton from their jackets, whistle a tune or examine

their finger-nails. Drakes preen themselves, which is probably how preening movements came to play such an important part in duck courtship behaviour.

At first, females probably identified their mates by distinctive types of preening behaviour, which have since been ritualized in the same way as the shoveler's mock feeding display. The male eider duck no longer bathes, but in his "bathing display", he merely twitches his bill in the water and then rolls his head back until his beak is pointing in the air. And the mandarin drake no longer preens behind his wing. Instead, he points with his bill to the hugely exaggerated fan feathers that have evolved as the unmistakable mark of his species, lifting them slightly to attract the full attention of his mate. He no longer preens, but thousands of generations of females have selected those males that have found the most convincing way of saying "I am a particularly fine mandarin drake".

Choosing the Right Species

Until recently, you could find a team of mules almost anywhere in the world, pulling a cart or a plough or carrying a load.

Mules are hybrids, the result of crossing a male African wild ass with the mare of a domestic horse (crossing a stallion with a female ass gives a different hybrid, called a hinny). Since horses have never lived wild in Africa, there is little chance that mules ever walked the Earth before our ancestors domesticated the wild ass and brought it to Asia. In nature, crosses between different species are rare. Only closely related animals that would not normally meet are likely to hybridize. Lions from Africa will mate with tigers from India if they are put together (the cubs are called tigons), but cheetahs and leopards, also from Africa, cannot be crossed with lions. Familiarity, it seems, breeds contempt and nothing more.

Like mules and hinnys, and the crosses between horses and zebras (zebroids), tigons are sterile. In other words, tigons, mules and zebroids cannot themselves have cubs or foals. In evolutionary terms, such offspring are a disaster, a lost opportunity for the parents to pass on some of their genes to future generations. Courtship helps animals avoid such disasters and ensures that they mate only with members of their own species, that is, with mates who will be able to produce young who in turn will be able to reproduce.

▶ Females tend to be choosy about their mates. For example, a female toad that mated with a male of the wrong species would waste an entire batch of eggs. Sperm, on the other hand, are relatively easy to make. A male can mate many times in a single season so for him a mistake is not nearly so serious. Perhaps it is just as well. This male common toad is attempting to mate with a carp.

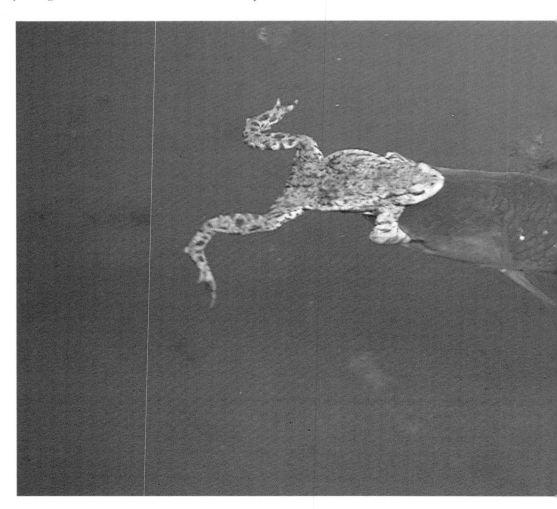

◀ A cross between a donkey and a zebra may be quite pretty, but in evolutionary terms it is a failure − a dead-end − as it cannot reproduce.

When two similar species of animal do live in the same place, their courtship routines make sure that they only mate with members of their own species. Birds and frogs often rely on the pitch and rhythm of their calls to tell each other apart. Also, when two similar species live in the same area, the females of both become more choosy about their partners, mating only with males whose song is clearly distinctive.

The Best Male Wins

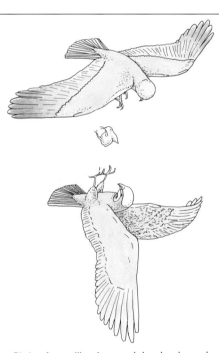

Birds of prey like the marsh harrier depend for survival on their skill as aerial hunters. As part of his courtship display, the male catches some prey and then flies to meet his partner. She flies beneath him, flicks over onto her back, and catches the food as he drops it. This intricate manoeuvre allows both birds to be sure of each other's flying skills.

Courtship is rather like an interview for a job. The job on offer is "mate", and because one male can often do the same job for many different females, it is the females who have the choice of mates. The first tests check that the candidates who apply are the right species, and that they are males. But once those vital preliminaries are out of the way, the female can concentrate on other details that will help her decide which male will make the best father for her young.

Hen harriers feed by catching small birds in mid-air, and their success depends on their spectacular flying ability. When hen harriers court, the male puts on a breathtaking display of aerobatics. He climbs high above the nest site, turns, and dives straight down until he is just above the ground. Then he levels out and climbs again to repeat the performance. Like most male birds, the male harrier will help to raise the chicks when they hatch, so showing how good he is at flying is a way of demonstrating that he will be fit and agile enough to feed the growing young.

A more direct test of the male's hunting ability would be to make him actually catch the food, and many female birds are not satisfied with mere showmanship but insist on results. A male tern must bring real food to his partner before she will mate with him. This benefits the female in two ways, because as well as being reassured of her potential mate's hunting ability, the food he brings her allows her to lay more eggs and so raise more chicks. If the male passes the test, he too will benefit by fathering more young, but if he does not bring enough food to satisfy the female, she is liable to go off with another male.

◀ Manakins are small, very active little birds that live on fruit and insects in the undergrowth and lower tree levels of the South and Central American forests. In the courtship season the males spend most of their time at traditional display sites, and for much of the day a pair of males will sing together from their tiny patch of forest. If they call loud and long enough, their song will eventually attract a female. The trio then move to a dance-perch on which the males perform a set of backward leapfrog hops, and elaborate display flights. The subordinate male then moves away discretely, leaving the dominant male to mate.

How such a system evolved is something of a mystery, but it may be that by helping a dominant male the subordinate male learns the courtship routine and stakes his claim to the display territory should his partner die.

◀ A male puffin brings food to his nest. The more food he brings, the better his chances will be that his chosen female will accept him as her mate. This form of courtship feeding is a test of how good the male is at providing food – and that information will help the female decide whether this particular male is a suitable father for her young.

A male bird usually stays with the female after mating and helps her to raise the chicks. In most other animals the male deserts the female immediately after mating, so his hunting skill will not help the young directly. But choosing a healthy mate is important for the female even if she never sees the male again. Her young will inherit half their genes from the father, and if he is carrying genes that make him susceptible to diseases or interfere with his ability to find food, then her young will be less likely to succeed in the struggle to survive.

▶ A male scorpion fly feeding on the body of a hoverfly. When the time comes for him to look for a mate, the scorpion fly's ability to find such insect carrion will be put to the test. If he fails to offer his partner a big enough meal, his attempts to mate with her will fail: she will reject him and go off in search of a better provider to be her mate.

The male scorpion fly stays with the female only long enough to mate, but like the male tern he first has to pass an interview that assesses his ability to find food. Scorpion flies are rather secretive insects that live in hedgerows and scrub. They are the vultures of the insect world, feeding on dead flies, bees, moths and butterflies. Before he can persuade a female to accept him for the job of mate, a male must find a suitable carcass – a scorpion fly delicacy that the female will enjoy. Only then is it worth his while to begin advertising for a mate, which he does by exposing his scent glands and releasing their special perfume. When a female arrives, she inspects the meal, and if it is to her taste she begins to eat. While she is feeding, she allows the male to mate with her. The bigger the meal the longer the mating, and the longer the mating, the more of her eggs the male fertilizes. In this way, the female allows males that are good at finding food to father more of her offspring.

The problem with this sort of test is that the female has no way of being certain that the male is always a good hunter. Even males with none of the characteristics she is looking for must get lucky and find a suitable carcass sometimes. Perhaps this is why many animals set their mates more subtle tests. Female guppies seem to prefer brightly coloured males as mates, and this turns out to be a surprisingly good way of testing the males' ability to find food. Guppies are small freshwater fishes, and because the males are pretty and colourful they

◀ The male octopus carries his sperm on one of his eight arms – a special one he uses to push the sperm into the female's reproductive opening. In some species the female may be able to judge the age of a male from the size of his sex organ. By choosing a big male she is selecting one that has lived for a long time and one that is therefore healthy, strong and well suited to the present conditions.

are often kept as pets in aquaria. The guppies' food contains only tiny quantities of the ingredients for the dyes that produce their bright colours, so only fish that are good at finding food ever succeed in dazzling a female.

Females that interview males for the job of mate ask questions that very often make little sense in human terms. It is far from obvious why a bowerbird with an impressive collection of stones or flowers, or a whale that can sing longer between breaths, should make an especially good father. But millions of years of evolution have made females into experts in the skills of the courtship interview. The questions may seem odd, but the answers always give the female crucial information about her suitor's qualifications as a potential mate.

Leking

Courtship is usually a very private affair, with a single male displaying to a female. But some animals are unwilling, or even unable, to court and mate unless they are surrounded by others of their own kind. For many seabirds, courtship takes place in large groups at traditional nesting colonies. This may be partly because there are few suitable nesting sites, but the birds do seem to choose to be in a dense group, ignoring other possible nesting sites that have not been colonized. Other animals take group courtship further and choose to gather together for courtship even though they later raise their young in isolation. There are numerous examples of birds, mammals, insects and amphibians that do this, and they provide some of the most curious sights in the natural world.

▲ At the start of the breeding season, male black grouse gather together at traditional leks or display grounds in order to display to the females that have gathered there.

The animals at these gatherings seem to play some bizarre game with an extremely complicated set of rules which only the players understand. The males stand, hang, perch or hover and perform some sort of display, while the females move between them passing judgement. To human eyes the performances all look much the same, and even with a complex array of video cameras, sound recorders, scales and tape measures, biologists can often find no reason why females choose to mate with one male rather than another.

These gatherings are called leks. Lek is a Swedish word that means "play", but for the males the lek is no game at all. Biologists may have difficulty in finding differences between the competing males, but the females have no problem in deciding who to mate with. Often the same male is chosen by nine out of every ten females, while many of the males never get the chance to mate at all. Even for the losers, there is no alternative but to keep trying because females will mate only at these gatherings. For the female, the lek is an excellent arrangement. It allows her to compare the merits of different males without having to waste her energy travelling great distances.

▼ Gannets always nest in extremely crowded conditions, usually in huge colonies on steep rocky cliffs. They are just one of many species that need other birds all around them in order to breed successfully.

Drugs and Love Potions

In Greek mythology Aphrodite was the goddess of love. Even though she was faithless and cruel, all men fell in love with her because she wore a magic girdle that made her irresistible. Aphrodite was always being asked to lend her girdle to other goddesses, either to bring back a straying husband or to entrap a young lover. She rarely agreed, because her girdle gave her such great power.

Mere mortals have long sought the power of Aphrodite's girdle – or at least something to do the same job. Brews, potions, charms and magic have all been tried by people desperate to win a lover. Drugs intended to have the effect of love potions are known as aphrodisiacs, after the goddess, but no one has ever found an aphrodisiac that really works on humans.

Animal aphrodisiacs, however, seem to be quite common. The African queen, for example, is one of the many butterflies that appear to use aphrodisiacs in their courtship. When the male finds a potential mate, he dusts the female with scent released from a bundle of hairs at

▶ The females of many heliconid butterflies are fertilized by waiting males as soon as they emerge from the pupal stage, sometimes even before their wings have dried. Once mated, they are seldom bothered by other males. The successful male transfers not only his sperm but also a pheromone that acts as an ''anti-aphrodisiac'' and discourages other males.

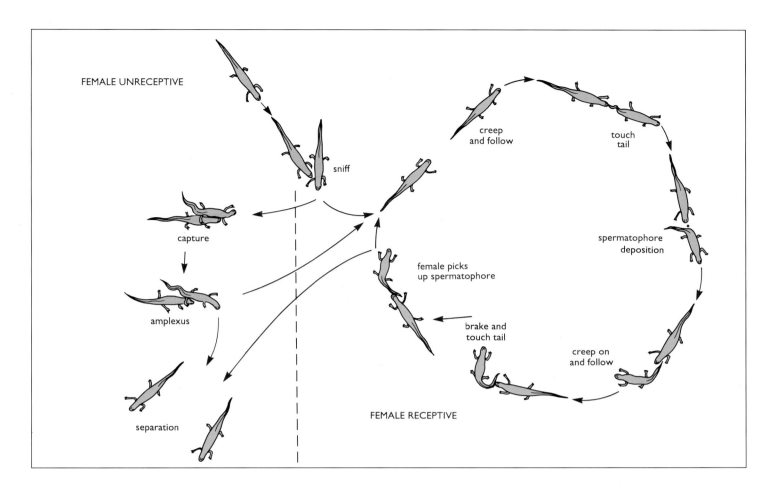

FEMALE UNRECEPTIVE

sniff

capture

amplexus

separation

creep and follow

touch tail

spermatophore deposition

female picks up spermatophore

brake and touch tail

creep on and follow

FEMALE RECEPTIVE

the tip of his abdomen. The scent apparently calms the female and prevents her from flying away, allowing him to settle beside her and mate. But is he really tricking a female into mating against her will? The African queen's scent seems to be an aphrodisiac, but it may not be working in quite the same way as Aphrodite's girdle. More likely the female butterfly uses the male's scent as a way of checking that he is healthy and the right species. To find animals that clearly use aphrodisiacs to change a female's behaviour we must look at newts, and in particular the red spotted newts of North America.

When newts mate, the male produces a small package of sperm known as a spermatophore, which has to be transferred to the female. Red spotted newts are common in the ponds of eastern North America, and they mate underwater. In order to transfer the spermatophore from the male to the female, both must cooperate in a complicated dance routine. If the female is willing to mate and does not try to escape from the male, this whole performance may take no more than a couple of minutes. But not all females are immediately receptive. If the chosen partner tries to escape, the male embarks on a second strategy of dosing her with aphrodisiac. He grabs her around the neck and begins to rub his cheek glands against her snout. These glands contain a mixture of drugs that slowly alter the female's behaviour. This process of drugging the female may take an hour or more, but eventually she is released, and once again the male resumes his courtship dance. The ploy is not always successful, and sometimes the female takes off immediately, never to be seen again. More usually, however, the aphrodisiac has the desired effect and the female eventually begins to respond to the male's advances.

▲ Courtship in red spotted newts can take one of two paths. If the female is receptive she will mate with the male almost as soon as he approaches her. If the female is unreceptive the male seizes her before she can run away, and then doses her with an aphrodisiac. This can completely alter the female's behaviour so that when she is released she responds to the male's courtship overtures.

Courting Disaster?

A female praying mantis is a killing machine. She has large eyes that are far better than ours at spotting anything that moves. When she sees an insect, she waits motionless until it is in range. Suddenly her front legs shoot out to grab her prey and drag it back to her powerful biting jaws. She is not very choosy about her food – a butterfly, a hornet, even another mantis can all expect the same treatment.

This behaviour creates a problem for the male mantis, who must get close enough to the female for mating without ending up as a meal. The male can do this in two ways. He can slowly creep towards the female and then, when he is close enough, take a flying leap on to her back. This method works if the female does not notice the male, but if he accidentally attracts her attention he may be grabbed and eaten. Most species of mantis mate like this, and the males just have to run the risks. The alternative is for the male to signal to the female and tell her that he is her intended suitor rather than an unknowing meal. Not many species do this but the Chinese mantis is one exception in which the male signals his intentions by waving his antennae and stamping.

Many spiders share with the mantis an approach to life that might be described as "eat first and ask questions later". Male wolf spiders avoid being attacked by their mates in much the same way as the male Chinese mantis, signalling from a distance with their strikingly marked palps. This is only one of many signals used by spiders. In one species, males present females with prey wrapped in silk – and then mate while the females are busy eating. Some crab spiders adopt a less romantic style and tie the female down with silk threads before attempting to mate with her.

For all these creatures, disarming the female is an essential part of courtship, but even so it is not unusual for males to be eaten while trying to mate. If they have mated successfully before they die, then at least they have succeeded in passing on their genes to the next generation. The meal they provide for the female could even help to make sure that their young get a good start in life. But if they fail to mate at all, this is simply nature's way of weeding out those animals that cannot follow the rules of courtship.

▲ The female praying mantis is a voracious killer that will eat insects her own size, and even bigger. To avoid being eaten before he has a chance to mate, the male must get his approach exactly right: one wrong move and he is dead. Even so, the male often ends up as a meal during or soon after mating. The one pictured here has been lucky, so far.

The Fairly Faithful Flycatcher

Most animals never see their partners again once they finish mating. At the other extreme, some birds use up so much energy rearing their young that the female is unable to raise even a single chick without help from the male. In these cases the pair must stay together throughout the breeding season if they are to raise any offspring. Birds that stay together like this can increase their breeding success with experience, and so the pair may stay together for life, becoming more successful every year. These long-term partnerships are most common among large birds, with swans and albatrosses providing famous examples of really faithful marriages.

▲ A male pied flycatcher with food for his young. This same male may well have another mate at another nest not far away, but she will receive no help at all in raising her brood. It is all part of the bird's complicated sexual strategy.

For some birds, however, the advantages of staying together may be less certain. If the female can raise more chicks with help from a male, she will do best if the male stays and helps her to raise her brood. But for the male, things may be different. If a female can raise even some of her young alone, the male may do better to court and mate with two females, and then help only one of them. The pied flycatcher is an example of a bird species in which the attractiveness of being faithful depends entirely on whether you are male or female.

Pied flycatchers are common woodland birds throughout northern Europe. A pair can expect to raise a clutch of five or six young in a breeding season, but a female deserted by her mate can usually only raise about three. A female will be most successful in raising young if she can ensure that her mate stays with her and helps to feed the brood. But for the male the best strategy is rather different. The most successful males are those that mate with one female and help her to raise her chicks, and also mate with other females and leave them to raise the young alone. In a single season they can father more than twice as many chicks as males that remain faithful to their first mates.

The result is that a male flycatcher wants to mate with as many females as possible. A female wants to check that her mate is being faithful to her, so she looks for guarantees. She will only mate with a male that courts her frequently over a long period of time. A male that does this is unlikely to be courting another female, but some females are still deceived. The breeding season is short, and females that lay eggs early in the season are more likely to be successful in raising young. For this reason, females may be hurried into mating before they are absolutely sure that the male has no other partners.

When the eggs have been laid, it is too late for the female to change her mind about her partner. Even if she could find another mate, the chances of raising more young from a late clutch are slim. When the female suspects that her mate is being unfaithful before she begins to lay, she may choose to abandon him, but this is by no means certain. Pied flycatchers nest in tree-holes, and good nest sites are rare. It may be worth mating with a male whose territory contains a good nest hole, even if he is already mated. A small brood secure from predators is better than a large brood that is killed before it fledges. The female pied flycatcher appears to make a complex series of choices in deciding on her mate, and is influenced by his song, his territory, and the likelihood of him having a second or even third mate.

▲ Swans usually remain faithful to each other not just for a single season but for life. The experience they accumulate by breeding together year after year helps them to work as a very efficient partnership – and that in turn enables them to raise more young in each successive season.

The Bulldog and the Peacock

Few of the animals exhibited in pet shows could ever survive for long in the wild. There are rabbits with ears so long they would trip over them if they tried to run, and pigeons that cannot fly. There are dogs with noses so short they can hardly breath, and mice so brightly coloured they would only be camouflaged in a paint shop. Release these prize-winners into the wild, and they will die. Any predator (except the flat-nosed dog) could catch the rabbit, and both the pigeon and the mice would be breakfast for a fox.

▶ By selective breeding over many years, humans have been able to produce animals that would stand no chance of survival in the wild. Natural members of the dog family, such as wolves and African hunting dogs, chase their prey until it is exhausted before closing in for the kill. With its short legs and distorted skull, the bulldog is barely able to move without gasping for breath. It could never hunt.

All these pets are the result of selective breeding. What happens is that in each generation, the breeder chooses the rabbits with the longest ears and allows them to mate together. After much effort and many generations, this has produced the creatures in the show. In the wild, of course, such freaks would soon be extinct, because natural selection makes sure that only animals that are efficient at finding prey and escaping predators survive. So how did natural selection produce the peacock, with his beautiful but very cumbersome tail?

The peacock's great tail makes him very conspicuous and a poor flyer. Peacocks are therefore much easier for predators to kill than the more "sensible" peahens. The peahen is a comparatively dull bird; greyish brown and inconspicuous. Her dull colours are an effective camouflage, particularly while she is sitting on her eggs. A peacock without his bright colours would doubtless live longer, but he would never mate. In nature, the peahen plays the same role as the animal breeder. She chooses as her mate a male with an impressive courtship display, ensuring that all her male chicks have the same long tails. Males succeed in passing on their genes only if they have tails long enough and gaudy enough to successfully court a mate, but still short enough for them to be able to fly away from predators.

◀ The shimmering colours and huge size of the male peacock's fully spread tail send messages to the female about his sex, his age and the state of his health. The more spectacular his display, the more likely the female is to select him to be the father of her young.

Charles Darwin was the first to realize that by choosing her partner in this way the female peacock could ensure the survival of traits like the peacock's tail, even though natural selection would favour males with shorter tails, or perhaps no tail at all. He called this "sexual selection" and suggested that it might explain the bright colours of many birds, the antlers of deer, and many other traits that might be a disadvantage in day-to-day survival.

For many years biologists doubted the importance of sexual selection, thinking that females had little opportunity to choose their mates and that male displays gave the females little useful information. After all, what advantage could it be to a peahen to have a beautiful mate if it means that her young are more likely to be eaten by predators? As the strange results of sexual selection are studied it becomes clear that displays do carry information to the female, and information that is vital to her selection of the best possible mate. They may indicate the strength of the male, his age, his ability to gather food or perhaps the fact that he has not succumbed to injury or illness. Now that more is known about the sort of things a male can tell a female with his courtship display, ideas are changing again. Well over a century after Darwin first published *On the Origin of Species*, more and more people have begun to think that he was probably right after all.

To Sing
or
Stay Silent

In one of his early silent films, Charlie Chaplin ended up fighting an enormous gorilla-shaped man in a boxing match. Just for good luck, Charlie put a horse-shoe inside one of his boxing gloves, and managed to win by a knock-out when a wild swing of the loaded glove caught the champion on the jaw. The little guy often won in silent movies, and audiences have always had a sneaky admiration for a clever cheat. The rules of courtship and mating are different from the rules of a boxing match: animals court and mate in a particular way because that is how their behaviour has evolved, not because someone has told them to. Animals can never really cheat, but the fight to find a mate is more important than any boxing match. Like Charlie Chaplin, many animals have found that there is more than one way to win a contest.

Field crickets make the Texas night noisy as they scratch out their courtship songs. The louder and longer a male sings, the more females he attracts, and the more successful he should be in the contest to father next year's crickets. So it was a great surprise when a researcher found that almost half the males do not sing at all. What he found was that these silent males stand quite close to a singing male and try to catch females on their way to mate with the singer.

By keeping quiet the silent males do not mate as often as the singers, *but they live longer*. This is because the grasslands of Texas are also home to a parasitic fly. This fly lays its eggs on the backs of crickets, and the larvae then eat their host alive. But the flies can find the crickets only if they hear them sing, so it is only singing crickets that die in this gruesome way. The flies keep a balance between the numbers of singing and silent crickets. Males that call do not live as long, but they mate more often. Males that stay silent live longer but mate only occasionally. On average, both raise the same number of young, and neither dies out.

Males quite often use such devious tactics when competing with each other, but females are not easily tricked. Courtship and mating are the most urgent tests for animals, so males might be expected to try all sorts of strategies, both fair and foul, to persuade the female to mate with them. Despite this, cheating in courtship is not common in the animal world. Successful females are the ones that are best at picking a successful father for their young. This is why females have become such good judges of the competing males, and good judges do not give first prize to a cheat.

◀▲ In the main photograph a parasitic tachinid fly sprays her larvae over the body of an unfortunate male cricket. The larvae will burrow into the cricket's body and devour it from inside, eventually killing it. In the smaller photograph above, one of the fly larvae has emerged again from the dead cricket and started to pupate.

SEX ROLES IN NATURE

Elephant seals provide a perfect example of the traditional view of male and female sex roles in nature. The huge males haul themselves ashore at the start of the breeding season and spend most of their time either sleeping or fighting among themselves. A week or so later the females arrive. They are much smaller than the males, and soon after they arrive each one gives birth to a single pup, which she feeds and protects as best she can.

With the arrival of the females, the males' aggressive behaviour increases. They roar, charge about, attempt to mate with every female in sight, and fight with any male who crosses their path, often wounding each other and crushing females and pups in the process. The whole performance is aimed at controlling and mating with the females.

However, there are many species in which these traditional roles do not apply, and where males share the work of parenthood with their partners — or even do most of the work. Like most things in nature the actual roles of the sexes often depend on the lifestyle of the individual species.

▶ Male northern elephant seals battle for supremacy on a crowded beach in California.

Fighting

▶ During the mating season, male wildebeest fight constant battles over the females in the herd. The fights are fierce and often end in injury to one or both of the animals, but wildebeest bulls very rarely fight to the death.

World War II pilots called their aerial battles "dog-fights", and on the ground the infantry were "fighting like tigers". Humans often talk of fighting in terms of animal-like behaviour, but it is worth remembering that only humans fight wars. Animals generally avoid serious fights. Carnivores that must kill for their food take pains to select prey that will not put up too much of a struggle. Squabbles between animals of the same species over food rarely result in more than a few scratches or ruffled feathers. It is usually better to look elsewhere for another meal than risk serious injury by fighting over food. But faced with a pack of hyenas attacking her calf, a female wildebeest will risk her own life to defend it. Even normally timid and docile animals will put up a fierce fight to protect themselves and their young.

A calf is the wildebeest's evolutionary investment in the future, and if there is a chance that she can save it then the mother will try. For the same reasons a male will fight for the chance to mate with a female and prevent others from mating with her. The males of many animals fight like this, and some of the most spectacular fights happen during the annual rut of the musk ox.

▲ Kangaroos may look rather comical but their fights are deadly serious. In this photograph two young male eastern grey kangaroos are sparring. In an all-out fight between adult males, skin and fur flies in all directions as the powerful animals leap at each other, kicking and slashing with their sharp claws.

The musk ox is a shaggy creature about the size of a bull which lives in the cold Arctic wastes of North America. Every autumn, as the females come into season, males fight each other for possession of a harem. Two males charge at each other from 100 to 130 feet (30 to 40 metres) apart, and collide head to head at full speed. They meet at something approaching 30 mph (50 km/h), and the noise can be heard for miles. These fights can kill, because if one of the contestants is stunned, the other may quickly turn and gore him in the side. Each year, a male musk ox has a one-in-ten chance of dying from wounds received while fighting.

For a male musk ox this risk is worthwhile. If he refuses to fight he has little chance of mating and will not pass on his genes to the next generation. Males that do not fight will quickly die out, and the best fighters will father the most calves. A female's needs are totally different from a male's. She only needs to mate once to be virtually certain that her eggs will be fertilized. The best way for a female to increase the number of offspring she produces is for her to eat as much as possible, and mate with the most successful male.

▲ It is not only the larger animals that fight over mates. Male stag beetles can inflict serious injuries on each other with their powerful jaws (used only in fights with rival males of their own species). After squeezing him hard and perhaps banging his head on the ground the victor will toss the loser aside and claim the disputed female as his mate.

A male must win these contests if he is to mate, but there is no point in young animals trying to take on bigger, stronger and older rivals. The best move for a young male is to avoid the risks of battle until he is strong enough to have a chance of success. Young males tend to keep clear of the fighting. Even when he does come to fight, a male may find himself losing and hopelessly outclassed. In that case it is generally possible for him to withdraw. Many animals have submissive signals which prevent hostilities – pointing their weapons away from their attackers, crouching down, or flattening their hair or feathers to make themselves look small. These signals are usually the opposite of challenging aggressive signals, and they save the loser. But the winner also benefits by observing the truce, because there is always a chance that even a dominant animal might injure himself in a fight with a subordinate. As a result, animals almost always keep their peace treaties.

Among red deer, rival stags use an additional tactic to reduce the danger of becoming involved in fights that they are certain to lose.

Instead of charging straight at their opponent as soon as they see him, they build up to the battle slowly. First they roar. A male defending a harem may roar every minute for two weeks during the rut. Any male wanting to challenge him starts by roaring back, and the two then begin a contest to see who can roar most frequently. Roaring is probably very tiring, and by keeping up a barrage of noise each stag literally "sounds out" the opposition, getting a good idea of which of them is more likely to tire first if it does come to a fight.

If the challenger keeps going, the two stags start marching across the heather, parallel to each other, about 30 feet (10 m) apart. This gives the two a good chance to size each other up, and again the challenger may well turn tail when he sees that the competition is bigger and stronger than he is. Only after half an hour of parallel marching do they fight, and because small males give up their challenge during the earlier rituals, fights are always between well-matched males, and they tend to be quite violent. All the preliminaries help to reduce the amount of fighting and injury, but they cannot avoid the dangers completely.

▲ The walrus is generally a fairly placid animal, but in the mating season the males' huge tusks are used as deadly weapons as they battle over the females. Both male and female walruses have tusks, and their size and shape provide other walruses with information about the owner's age, sex and status.

Males That Avoid Fights

Females benefit by mating with the winner of a fight because their young will inherit genes that made the victor strong and healthy. The males that win fights do even better because they end up mating often and fathering a large number of young. It is the losers that have a problem. If they simply accept their failure they end up with no mates, but fighting is not the only way to win the battle for fatherhood.

When a red deer stag roars across the mountains, opponents roar back at him to challenge him for his entire harem of females. These "honest" stags are his greatest threat. If they defeat him in battle they will take over his harem and mate with all his females. But he must also look over his shoulder, where there is another threat.

In every herd of red deer there are a few males that never develop antlers. These are known as hummel deer, and because they carry no antlers they cannot fight, so they cannot compete with the dominant stags to hold a harem. With no antlers, they are also of no value to sportsmen, and for centuries game-keepers have been trying to cull them from their herds. With both these problems it is amazing that a single hummel deer survives. But they do survive, and that is because of their decidedly sneaky sexual behaviour.

Antlers are a mark of the stag's sex, so a harem master is continuously on the look-out for animals with antlers near his harem. Without antlers a hummel can move between harems without being spotted by the harem master. While the harem master is engaged in a bout of roaring or a fight with a rival, the hummel will mate with a receptive hind, and then quietly move on to find another female. A

◀ A dominant red deer stag is surrounded by his harem of hinds during the rut. He will mate with most of them, but must spend a great deal of time and energy keeping the hinds together and fighting off challenges by rival males.

harem master is reasonably certain to mate with most of his harem, but fighting and roaring drain his energy and he is unlikely to hold a large group of hinds for more than a few seasons. A hummel does not fight at all, unless he is caught in the act and is forced to defend himself, and so he is usually in better condition than the stags. He probably lives longer, and he can increase the number of hinds he meets by moving among the harems of several other males. His sneaky tactics are remarkably successful.

The stag and the hummel are quite different to look at, even though both are males of the same species. When there is more than one way for a male to mate successfully, such differences are common. Male digger bees fight in bundles around a female as she emerges from her pupation burrow. It is virtually always the largest male that is successful in these scrambles, carrying the female off to a nearby tree to mate with her. But some females emerge from their burrows without being noticed by males. These females fly off and begin feeding on the surrounding flowers, and would perhaps remain unpaired if other males of the same species did not have a completely different method of finding their mates. These males are much smaller, and would have no chance in the free-for-all fight that usually develops around an emerging female. Instead they fly around the edge of the area or wait perched in the surrounding trees. They attempt to mate with every female that comes past, and although most have already been fertilized by larger males, there are always a few that have slipped through the net and are still unmated.

Reversing the Sex Roles

▶ The male variegated fairy-wren of Australia has the brilliant plumage and bright, cocky, aggressive character that is typical of the normal male sex role in birds.

The usual picture we have of courtship and breeding among animals is of big, brightly-coloured males dancing, displaying or fighting for the females. Then, after mating with one of these handsome creatures, the smaller and rather dull-looking females go off to produce and look after the young.

This is explained by the fact that females put much more energy into producing young than males do, so they have more to gain from ensuring the safe survival of those offspring. Males, on the other hand, can breed more successfully by mating with as many females as possible. But with plenty of males around, each one must fight for a female or woo her, persuading her by his courtship displays that he is the best possible father for her young. This is why males are usually bigger, stronger, and more brightly coloured than females, and it is usually the males of a species that make the first moves in courtship. Usually – but not always.

◀ Despite its misleading name the seahorse is a fish. It uses the fin on its back for swimming and its curled tail for clinging to weed stems. Most unusually, it is the male who cares for the eggs. As soon as the female releases them the male catches them in his pouch and from then on they are his responsibility. When the eggs have completed their development and hatched, the father "squirts" the tiny living seahorses out of the pouch. This reversal of the normal parent roles causes a similar reversal in the fishes' courtship. Male seahorses can only care for one batch of eggs at a time, so a male ready and able to receive eggs is always in demand. The result is that it is the female who has to do the courting. She must find a "free" male and persuade him to accept her eggs before his pouch is filled with the eggs of a rival female.

Wilson's phalarope is a dainty wading bird that breeds across a vast area of the northern United States and southern Canada. Unusually, the female is much more brightly coloured than the male, with a striking black stripe running across her eyes and down the sides of her neck, separating her white throat and russet-brown fore-neck from a pearly-white crown and nape. The male, by contrast, is drab, grey-brown, and inconspicuous.

Female phalaropes not only look like male birds, they behave like males too. Early in the season, males and females pair up, and the female then defends her mate against any competition that swims too close. First she threatens, ruffling her feathers and lunging towards the intruder. This is no idle bluff. Any trespassing bird that fails to take notice and leave quickly will be attacked mercilessly. Female phalaropes have been seen standing on top of their rivals in the water, pecking viciously at the backs of their heads.

The females also take the lead in courtship. As the breeding season begins, males swim nervously around the edges of their ponds, often pursued by several females. If the male takes off from the surface of the pond, an aerial chase follows during which the males swoop low over other birds on the water, encouraging other females to join in.

So what is the male phalarope's secret? Almost every other male in the natural world must risk his life trying to find and court a mate, and many are unsuccessful. But for the male phalarope the problem is quite the opposite. He runs a real risk of being injured as a result of the tussles between his prospective partners. The answer is that male Wilson's phalaropes invest much more than most birds in the care of their young. Although the female helps to excavate their scanty nest, she abandons the eggs immediately they are laid and takes no further

part in the proceedings. It is the males that must brood the eggs, for almost three weeks, and then lead the chicks to water where they will learn to feed.

In a sense, the phalarope is the exception that proves a fundamental rule of animal behaviour. It is not necessarily the male that is big and brightly coloured for dancing, displaying or fighting. This role is taken on by whichever parent provides least for the young, whether it is the male or the female. The parent that does most of the work is likely to be smaller, to have more subdued colouring, and to take a less active part in courtship. The more help the males of a species provide, the more intense is the competition between females for their services. This trend reaches its climax in creatures like the phalarope, in which the normal sex roles are completely reversed.

◀ The pheasant-tailed jacana is one of only a few species of bird in which the sex roles are reversed. In this species the female is very pugnaceous, and will defend her territory against any other female that comes near her mate. The male incubates the eggs and cares for the young when they hatch. One reason for this arrangement may be that jacana nests are flimsy, and easily destroyed by floods or predators. If she is free of other duties, the female is able to feed up and be ready to lay a second clutch if the first one is lost.

Females in Competition

Battles between males are so spectacular and so familiar that it is easy to forget that females also fight. Anyone who has ever watched a flock of hens has probably noticed that they do not live in peaceful harmony. Their fights are not usually very bloody or dramatic, but hens do fight, and they maintain their status in the flock by regularly picking on the weaker birds lower down the pecking order. Introduce a new bird to a flock of hens, and she will amost certainly lose a few feathers in squabbles before she finds her place in the hierarchy.

Fights between females are most often over food rather than directly related to breeding. The reason for this is that fighting usually stems from competition, and females do not usually have to compete for their mates. A single male can fertilize many females, so all the females are sure of mating. As a result, the females of most species have no reason to fight over males.

Even so, competition between females can still influence the number of young they succeed in raising. A female at the bottom of the pecking order will be the first to go hungry when food is scarce, and with less food available to supply her needs she is forced to devote less time and energy to raising her young. By keeping her subordinates in

▼ The chickens in a farmyard flock may seem peaceful enough, but this harmony is usually achieved only after a succession of fierce struggles for dominance among the hens.

their place, the dominant female gets first pick at the food herself, and so reduces the number of young that will be born to compete with her own offspring.

Animals that live in colonies and share the work of raising the young often show the effects of competition between females much more clearly. One such creature is the groove-billed ani, a South American bird of the cuckoo family. Groove-billed anis live in groups of up to four pairs, sharing a single territory and nest. All the females in a group lay their eggs in the same nest, and all help to incubate them. At first sight it appears that far from competing against each other, the females cooperate and help to raise each other's young. But the broken eggs on the ground beneath the nest tell a rather different story. The females have a strict hierarchy, and when the breeding season begins the lowest-ranking female is the first to lay. The other birds follow in order, with the dominant female laying her eggs last. Before she lays, she makes several visits to the nest, each time tossing out one of the eggs of the other birds. By doing this she makes sure that the final clutch will not be so large that it cannot be incubated properly, and also that most of the eggs in it will be her own.

▼ The ostrich provides a classic case of role reversal. Several females lay their eggs in the same large nest where they are incubated by a single male. However, the females are not all equal in rank. The senior females place their eggs near the centre of the nest where they are most likely to hatch successfully.

Changing Sex

The sex of a human being is decided at the moment he or she is conceived, and the deciding factor is the type of sperm that happens to fertilize the egg. If the fertilizing sperm is of one type the baby will be a girl, and if it is of the other type, it will be a boy. The sex of humans, and indeed of all mammals and birds, is determined by their genes, but this is not the case for all animals. Some animals can even change sex during their lifetime, male and female depending not on the creature's genes but on its age or size.

One animal that changes sex in this way is the slipper limpet. Slipper limpets are shellfish, originally from the coasts of North America but now also found in European waters following their accidental introduction along with American oysters. They are quite a common sight, usually washed up on the beach in a clump. At the bottom of each cluster is the largest shell, with smaller and smaller ones piled on top. The result is a curved pile of shells, and these piles are actually mating stacks. The big ones at the bottom are the females, and the smaller, younger ones are males. But as he gets bigger and older, a male changes into a female, and new males start attaching themselves to her.

Changing sex like this gives a slipper limpet the best of both worlds. When it is small it does not have much spare energy for mating, so it produces sperm which are small and easy to make. The sperm do not have a very great chance of being successful because there are several small males riding on the back of each female, but it is worth the small effort it takes to make them because meanwhile the limpet can continue to grow. When it grows bigger, a slipper limpet can feed much more efficiently, so it can afford to put more of its effort into reproduction. Then, it is worth making the much larger effort of producing eggs, and eggs virtually guarantee success for the animal that can afford to produce them. So larger slipper limpets reproduce more successfully if they are female, and this explains the sex change they undergo.

◀ The tentacles of sea anemones are armed with stinging cells capable of killing most small fish, but clownfish are immune to the poison and even seek protection among the anemone's waving arms. Several fish live around each anemone, and all but the largest are males. If the female dies, within a few days the next-largest fish will change sex and take over the role of resident female.

▼ In a "stack" or "chain" of slipper limpets, only the large one at the bottom is female. The smaller shellfish stacked on top are all younger – and all are males.

Hermaphrodites: the Best of Both Worlds

▲ The courtship dance of the Roman snail is strangely beautiful as the creatures entwine their bodies. It is also extremely productive since this single mating will result in both animals producing fertilized eggs.

On warm, humid nights, garden slugs dance their elegant courtship. Slowly they circle each other, sliding forward on silvery trails, until eventually the two slimy ribbons join and the two slugs mate. But which is the male and which the female? The confusing answer is that both of them are both. Slugs are hermaphrodites, which means that each individual is male and female at the same time. A lot of other garden animals are like slugs in this respect. Worms, snails and most plants have male and female parts on the same individual, and there are two good reasons for this.

Travelling flat out, an eager snail can cruise at about 6 feet (2 m) an hour. A slug can manage roughly the same dizzying pace, and except on cool, damp nights, neither slugs nor snails can travel far before they start to dry out and die. All this seriously limits their ability to search for mates. If such slow-moving creatures were not hermaphrodites, the males would gain very little by trying to race around the garden fertilizing females, simply because they are unable to race anywhere. As hermaphrodites, slugs, snails, worms and plants benefit in several ways. If a worm was only one sex, half the worms it met would be the same sex as itself, and no good for mating with. So on average, two encounters would produce only one batch of fertilized eggs.

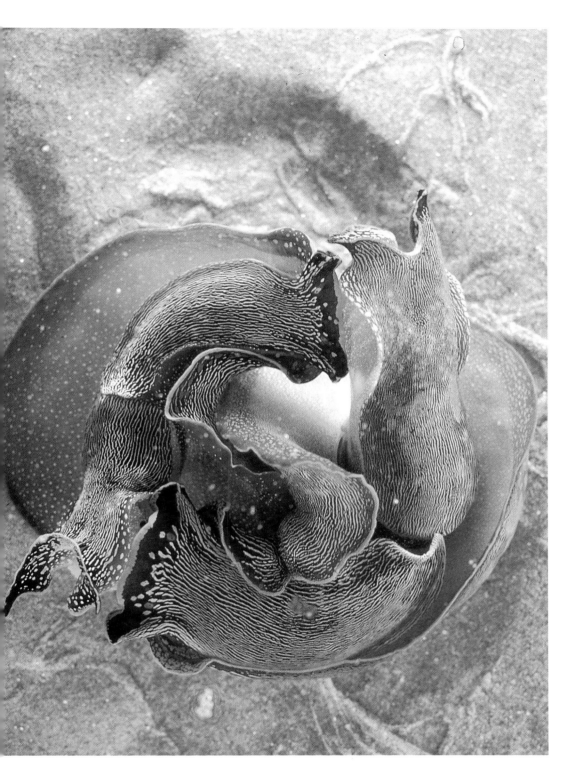

◀ Sea slugs are much bigger and very much more colourful than ordinary land slugs, yet they reproduce in much the same way. Like all slugs, and most snails and worms, they are hermaphrodites so both animals in a pair are fertilized when they mate.

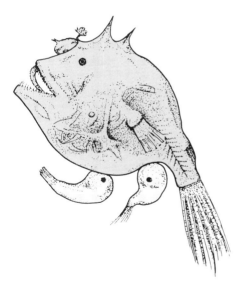

▲ Very few fish live in the dark depths of the ocean but this is the home of the angler fish, which carries a luminous lure to attract prey within reach of its powerful jaws. To ensure that it always has a mate when breeding time comes around, the large female carries one or more tiny males around with her – attached to her body where they live as parasites.

Worms are hermaphrodites, so every time one bumps into another they are potential mates, and their efforts are rewarded. In fact, the success of an encounter like this is even better than simply guaranteeing that the two can mate. It means that for each and every meeting, *two* batches of eggs can be fertilized – one batch from each worm. This compares with *one* batch being fertilized as a result of *two* encounters if each worm were only one sex. So encounters between worms are four times as productive as they would be if the animals were not hermaphrodite, which is good news for gardeners. Unfortunately, exactly the same system of reproduction is found in slugs and snails, which is definitely bad news for gardeners.

▶ To attract a pollinator, a plant must provide some kind of reward, and this usually takes the form of pollen or nectar. It must also "spend" precious energy on growing petals and other structures to guide the pollinator to the right part of the plant. Hermaphrodite plants get the best value for the effort they put in by using the same arrangement of flower parts to fertilize their seed with pollen from other plants, and to distribute their own pollen to other plants.

Being hermaphrodites allows slow-moving animals to make the most of each mating opportunity. There are also other advantages to being both sexes at the same time. Plants do not have to meet for fertilization to happen. Instead, the pollen is carried from the male to the female by the wind, by insects, birds or some other animal. Because the plant is hermaphrodite a bee can collect and deposit pollen at the same time, and so, rather like the worms, every meeting is doubly productive. But this does not explain why wind-pollinated plants are hermaphrodite. They simply shed their pollen into the air and it is blown to the female flower of another plant.

Once flowers have been pollinated, the colourful petals fade and drop off and the male parts of the flower wither and die. Only the fertilized female parts survive, and they grow to produce the seeds and the fruit. During the mating season, a hermaphrodite plant or animal can put most of its energy into its male effort and produce lots of pollen or sperm. After fertilization, there is very little for a normal single-sex male to do, but a hermaphrodite does not face that problem. It can switch all its energy to its female effort, and so help its offspring to survive and thrive. It is a very efficient system.

DOING WITHOUT SEX

Sex is an amazingly complicated business. Animals that reproduce sexually must make special cells — the eggs and the sperm. For this they need special organs, the ovaries and testes. They must take risks in finding a partner of the opposite sex. They must spend time and energy courting and mating. In fact, sex is such a performance that it is hardly surprising to find that a great many animals do without it all together.

Many of the animals that reproduce without sex have the advantage of being able to reproduce very quickly, and this often enables them to take over when slower-breeding competitors are still trying to establish themselves. The strange thing is that most creatures that reproduce without sex, like the freshwater hydra opposite, can also breed sexually — and this gives them the best of both worlds.

▶ The freshwater hydra normally reproduces without sex, by a simple budding process, but the animal is able to switch to sexual reproduction if the conditions in its pond start to deteriorate.

Asexual Reproduction

Reproducing without sex is called asexual reproduction, and the simplest asexual reproduction is found in the simplest forms of life. Thousands of these tiny living things may be swimming about in a single drop of pond water. We cannot normally see them, but even a small microscope can open up this world to us. Some of these creatures are plants, the algae, which use their green pigment to trap the Sun's energy. Others are animals, feeding on the plants or on decaying animal and plant debris in the water. Some are neither plant nor animal, but half-way between the two. Like plants they are green with chlorophyll, but like animals they swim or slither from place to place.

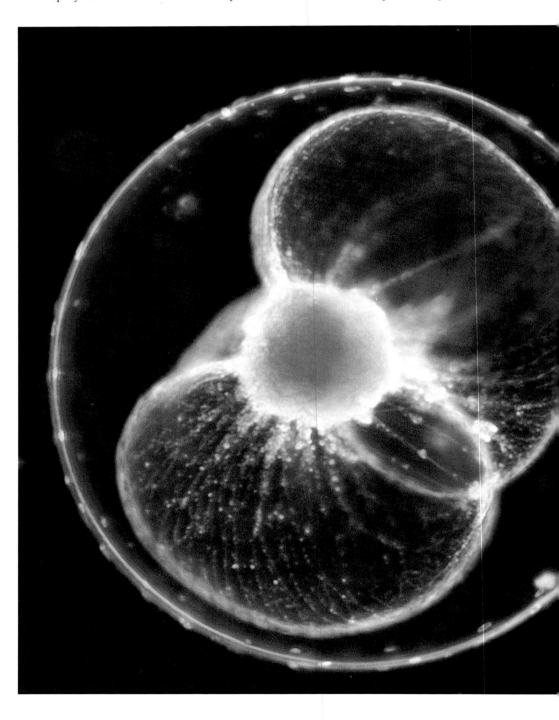

▶ Microscopic single-celled organisms such as these dinoflagellates often reproduce simply by splitting in two. The cell nucleus first divides to produce two complete new nuclei. The cell itself then divides in two, with each part containing a brand new nucleus carrying a complete set of the coded instructions it needs to function independently. Like many primitive organisms, the dinoflagellates lie part-way between animal and plant. They function like animals but can also carry out photosynthesis – the chemical process that enables plants to harness the energy of the Sun. Because of this they are an important part of the marine food chain, providing food for a host of other sea creatures.

Many of these creatures never reproduce sexually at all. In the simplest of them each individual is just a single cell with a single nucleus. To reproduce itself it divides in the same way as any other cell. First the nucleus splits in half, and then the creature breaks into two parts. Finally the two halves separate, and two new individuals are produced – each with its own nucleus, the cell's control centre.

It is very efficient for a creature to reproduce by just splitting in two, and many of the tiny organisms in pond water have been breeding successfully like that for hundreds of millions of years. No time is wasted on courtship or mating, and no energy is wasted on producing sperm or eggs. Each animal is able to reproduce, and so the numbers can grow twice as fast as is possible in animals that must have both males and females in order to breed.

The process of reproducing just by splitting in half is easiest for

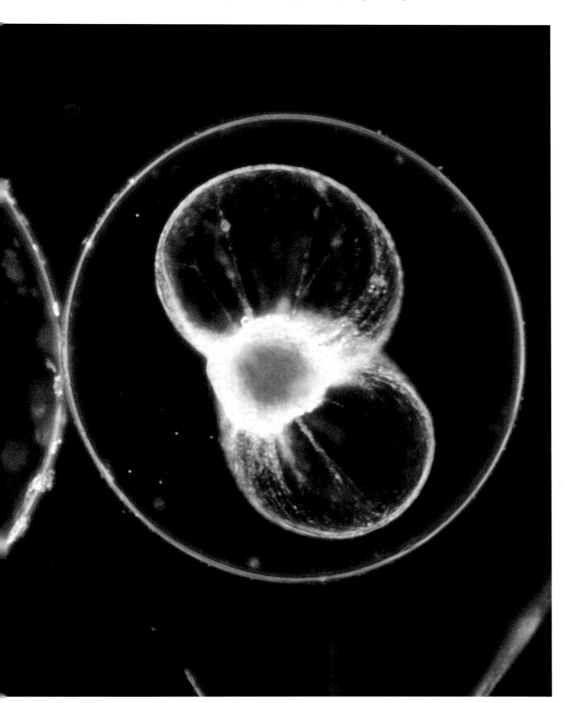

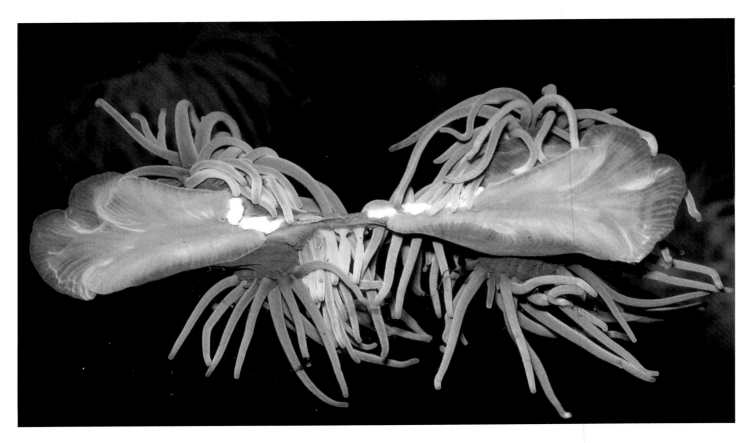

▲ A snakelock anemone reproducing in one of the simplest ways imaginable – by splitting in half. As organisms become more complex, with specialised organs for different functions, this simple solution becomes impractical.

simple, single-celled animals, but a few larger animals that are made up of a number of different cells also manage to multiply themselves in this way. Some flatworms reproduce simply by splitting off bits of their bodies. The two flatworms that result regrow the bits that are missing and become complete worms. Sea anemones can reproduce in much the same way, some species splitting in half while others grow miniature versions of themselves like tiny buds around their bases.

Although asexual reproduction is most common among very simple animals, even some of the most complicated plants use it too. If the branch of a living tree gets bent down and touches the ground, roots may spring out from it and produce a new tree. A potato plant develops potatoes that survive through the winter, and next year each one grows into a new plant that has been produced asexually. Rose bushes frequently produce new stems, known as "suckers", from their roots, and these then grow into new plants.

▶ When single-celled creatures split, the nucleus must first divide very precisely: the rest of the animal then divides into roughly equal parts. In flagellates such as *Euglena* (1) the animal divides lengthways. In ciliates such as *Tetrahymena* (2) the smaller micronucleus must also divide, and a new "mouth" groove has to form. In the simple *Amoeba* (3) there are no complications: once the nucleus has divided, the body can split anywhere.

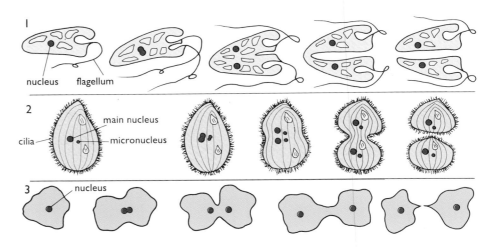

Asexual reproduction is very common in plants, but most of them can also reproduce sexually. Similarly, most of the animals that reproduce asexually can reproduce sexually as well. This is because asexual reproduction has one important drawback. Offspring that are produced asexually are bound to have exactly the same set of chromosomes as their parents. They will be adapted to the same conditions as their parents, and be susceptible to the same diseases. Sexual reproduction produces offspring that are slightly different from their parents, and these slight differences make it possible for them to succeed in slightly different conditions. So sexual reproduction has quite important advantages, but the creatures in the pond prove that reproducing asexually can also be extremely successful.

◄ The spider plant reproduces by growing miniature copies of itself on the end of long tendrils. In the wild, these would take root when they touched the ground, and would then develop into new plants. Spider plants also produce small, inconspicuous flowers which enable the plant to reproduce sexually as well.

Parthenogenesis or "Virgin Birth"

There are two unusual things about the stick insects that live in southern Britain. The first is that both species were accidentally introduced from New Zealand. The second is that they are all female, and these facts are connected. If the first lonely immigrant stick insect had been a male there would have been no descendants. If it had been a female that reproduced normally the outcome would have been the same. But these stick insects do not breed normally. They are asexual, and it is common for colonizers to be so.

▲ A stick insect from southern Europe. Males of this species are extremely rare, and most of the females reproduce by laying unfertilized eggs, which hatch into identical copies of themselves. It is a perfectly good system while conditions remain suitable for the insect, but if the environment changes the species may find it difficult to adapt and survive.

Animals such as insects cannot reproduce asexually by budding because they are too complex. Each part of the body is specialized for a particular function. Reproduction is the function of sex organs, and the way these stick insects have managed to become asexual is by changing the way in which their eggs are produced.

Eggs containing living embryos are not produced in the usual way, after fertilization by the male, but develop on their own, inside the female, without ever being fertilized. The young stick insect which emerges inherits all its chromosomes from its mother. It is genetically identical to her, and so of course is female.

The Whiptail Lizard

▲▼ "Mating" between asexual whiptail lizards mimics true mating in one of the parent species (below).

The southwest of the United States is dry desert country with tall cacti, and is home to a wealth of snakes and lizards. Small and relatively inconspicuous amongst the gila monsters and rattlesnakes are a group of lizards called the whiptails. There are several species, but one is particularly interesting because it has no males. Without being fertilized, the females' eggs hatch into identical copies of their mothers.

How does such a creature evolve? Were there once males that became redundant when the females managed to reproduce on their own? In the case of the asexual whiptail, the answer is no. By studying the chromosomes of all the species in the area, biologists have worked out that the asexual whiptail is actually a cross between two of the other species. The first female capable of breeding on her own must have been produced when a male of one species mated with a female of the other by mistake.

Mating between different species produces hybrids. These rarely survive, and those that do are usually infertile, like the mule. But the hybrid whiptail lizard turned out to be extremely unusual. It is able to breed asexually as its eggs are capable of developing and producing healthy young without ever being fertilized by sperm. Even more remarkable is that the female whiptails court each other and engage in pseudo-copulation — that is, they go through the entire performance of courtship and mating except, of course, that since they are both female they cannot actually mate. The result of this odd behaviour is quite surprising. Lizards that take the female role in pseudo-copulation eventually lay more eggs than those that have not gone through the "courting" and "mating" performance.

The Generation Game

▲ By reproducing without mating, throughout the summer, aphids can multiply at an astonishing rate.

Greenfly are the scourge of rose growers. Every summer there comes a day when suddenly the plants are smothered in these tiny pests. Thousands appear as if from nowhere, sucking the sap from the growing tips of shoots and disfiguring the buds that days before promised such a wonderful display of flowers. The greenfly are not only unsightly. As they pierce the plant's stem to feed on its sap, they inject viruses that may ultimately do even more damage.

Greenfly belong to a group of plant pests known as aphids. There are many different species, but there are few plants that escape their attentions. Some plants are particularly susceptible; a field of broad beans might have 2,000,000,000 black bean aphids living in a single acre (0.4 hectare).

Black bean aphids can reproduce so quickly and reach such vast numbers partly because there are no males. Each aphid is entirely self-sufficient, able to reproduce itself without any help. Inside the insect, the unfertilized eggs simply develop and grow into identical miniature copies of their mother. Every day, each adult aphid gives birth to another live offspring. It takes about four or five days for this young aphid to mature, and then it too starts to breed. The rapid growth in aphid numbers that depresses farmers and gardeners is possible because there are no males to waste space and food, and the females need spend no time mating.

The aphids, however, do not have things all their own way. Ladybirds and hoverfly larvae eat them. Tiny parasitic wasps come and lay their eggs on them. These predators are the gardener's friends, but they can never do more than keep the aphid numbers in check. The aphids breed so fast that their enemies can never keep up with them. Ladybirds, hoverflies and the parasitic wasps all breed sexually, and cannot increase their numbers at the same dizzying rate as the aphid population.

Like all animals that breed by parthenogenesis, aphids have the great advantage that they can produce an enormous population very quickly. The disadvantage is that every individual in that population is bound to be just the same as all the others. The aphids wait until autumn before beginning to tackle this problem. As the beans begin to die, the aphids fly to nearby trees where they lay the batch of eggs that will survive the winter. The last aphid generation of the summer is different from those that have gone before. It consists of males as well as females. These mate — and because the eggs that result are produced by sexual reproduction, they will produce a variety of different individuals that will be able to survive in a whole range of different conditions.

Aphids repeat this pattern every year. They produce a series of generations by parthenogenesis, and then produce one generation sexually. Using both methods of reproduction gives them the best of both worlds, which is why they are so amazingly successful.

The development of unfertilized eggs in this way is called parthenogenesis, sometimes known as "virgin birth" because a female produces young without ever mating. Although parthenogenesis is commonest among insects, it does occur in other groups of animals as well. Very rarely, even the eggs of animals that do not normally reproduce in this way fail to divide properly and can begin to develop. Usually the young animal dies at a very early stage, but frogs and even turkeys have occasionally grown to maturity from unfertilized eggs.

Breeding parthenogenetically has obvious advantages to an animal. First, it makes it possible to breed without all the time-wasting effort of finding a mate. For something that moves as slowly and as rarely as a stick insect this may be important. The second advantage is that a parthenogenetic species does not have to produce males, only females, and every one of those females can breed, so the size of the population can grow twice as fast as it could for an animal that breeds sexually. And there is another advantage. If the animal is successful, it is far better to produce identical copies as offspring than to tamper with the genetic recipe. Sexual reproduction mixes the genes of males and females so that none of the young are exactly like either parent. If the mother is perfect, why change? However, there is a risk involved as we have seen. If the climate, food supply or other conditions change, the species may not be able to cope — and it has no way of evolving to meet the new challenge.

Asexual reproduction gives animals so many advantages that for many years scientists puzzled over exactly why animals bother to reproduce sexually. There are many subtly different explanations, but central to them all is the idea that no mother ever is perfect, or at least if she is, she cannot stay that way for long. As the climate changes, or new diseases invade the population, or she moves to a new location, she will be less well adapted to the new situation. Animals that reproduce sexually give birth to a variety of offspring, and there is at least a chance that one will be better adapted than either of its parents to the changed surroundings.

The Double Life of the Jellyfish

Anyone who has ever walked along a beach will be familiar with jellyfish. In some places they are very common, and although most species are small, some can reach 3 metres or more in diameter, with tentacles 30 metres long. They are carnivorous creatures, catching their prey with special stinging cells located on the tentacles. These can inflict a painful sting if you are unfortunate enough to swim against one of the larger species, but you can safely feel the stinging cells of this kind of animal by placing your finger among the waving arms of the jellyfish's close relative the sea anemone.

One of the many strange things about the creatures is that most of them have two completely different stages in their life-cycle. One reproduces sexually; the other reproduces asexually. Generally, the sexual stage swims freely in the sea but in the asexual stage the animal is permanently fixed to a rock underwater. As the asexual stage feeds and grows, it splits into sections until it looks like a stack of tiny plates. The biggest "plate", at the top, has tentacles and catches food particles as they drift by, but eventually it breaks off and swims away. The next plate in the stack then grows tentacles. It too feeds for a while, and then breaks off and swims away – and so on. Once separated, the free-swimming section grows into the familiar jellyfish. Eventually it develops sexual organs producing sperm or eggs which are released into the water. Each egg that is fertilized develops into a larva, which (if it survives) settles on a rock and becomes the start of a new asexual "stack of plates" – so completing the full cycle.

Sea anemones are related to jellyfish but they have become specialized to live as adults attached to rocks. They produce eggs or sperm inside their bodies: some species then release the eggs and sperm into the water where they combine to form free-swimming larvae. In other species the eggs are fertilized inside the female's body.

To add to this complexity, there are some species of jellyfish in which the swimming sexual form becomes attached to a rock and one related group in which the sexual form produces a gas-filled balloon and floats away! This group includes the most famous of all jellyfish, the Portuguese Man-of-War. These animals are very ancient and very simple: their life-cycle may be strange, but it is worth remembering that they have been successful for many millions of years – and that is an impressive record for any form of animal life.

▶▶ The medusa or free-swimming stage of the common jellyfish *Aurelia aurita* is found throughout the Mediterranean and North Atlantic. It grows to about 25cm in diameter and swims with a pulsating motion produced by rhythmical contractions of the muscles in its semi-transparent dome-shaped body.

▶ The diagram here shows in simplified form the stages of development from the asexual sedentary stage of the jellyfish's life-cycle through to the sexual free-swimming medusa stage. The sedentary stage develops from a fertilized egg. It is attached to the seabed and reproduces initially by budding. Each of the new sedentary organisms then develops into a vertical stack, from which miniature free-swimming jellyfish break off and swim away as they mature. These medusae then develop into adult jellyfish which reproduce sexually to produce a new generation of sedentary hydroids.

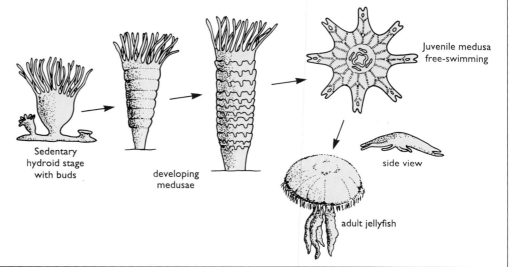

Sedentary hydroid stage with buds

developing medusae

Juvenile medusa free-swimming

side view

adult jellyfish

FROM CASTAWAYS TO CARRYCOTS

In nineteenth-century Russia there lived a woman who still holds the record as the world's most prolific mother. When she died in 1856 she had given birth to a total of 69 children — 16 pairs of twins, 7 sets of triplets, and 4 sets of quadruplets. It is not known how many of her children survived, or what she died from, but most parents would guess that it must have been exhaustion.

For one woman to have 69 babies is impressive, but it is nothing compared with the productivity of some animals. A female oyster produces over 100 million eggs in each batch, and she may release several batches during a single summer. The important difference is that the oyster simply releases her eggs into the water and then does absolutely nothing more for them. The human mother has embarked on a full-time task lasting for many years.

▶ Unlike our common frog, which abandons its eggs to chance, the glass frog of Central America sticks its eggs to a leaf overhanging a pond or stream and guards them until they hatch and the tadpoles drop into the water below.

Tackling Parenthood

Humans and oysters are exact opposites in their approach to parenthood. Modern humans generally have fewer offspring than any other species of animal, and look after them for longer than any other animal. We make careful parents. Oysters come close to the record for the highest productivity, but then they take no care of their offspring at all. They are "careless" parents. This, however, is not the same as saying that they are bad parents. Oysters are very common, so they must be successful breeders. Their careless method of parenting clearly works, and it is not only oysters that breed like this. Many sea animals do absolutely nothing for their young. They just release their eggs and sperm into the water. Many of the eggs are never even fertilized, while those that are successfully fertilized develop into larvae that must swim off immediately and fend for themselves.

▲ Like many sea creatures, mussels simply release their eggs and sperm into the sea. They leave it to chance and the water currents to fertilize their eggs, and take no part at all in raising their young.

Producing young and looking after them takes a great deal of time and effort. Animals tend to concentrate either on producing large numbers of young, or on caring for a smaller number, and which of these alternatives an animal employs depends on its structure, its habitat, and the way it lives. Each species adopts the method that allows it to produce the greatest number of surviving offspring.

From where an oyster sits, there is little alternative to breeding the way it does. The female is stuck to a stone in the sea, and her young have to get themselves stuck to a stone somewhere else in the sea. Nothing she can do will help them in their dreadfully dangerous journey in search of a resting place. Most of them will simply not find anywhere to settle, and her best strategy is to be so productive that by sheer overwhelming numbers it is almost certain that one or two of her millions of eggs will survive the journey and land on a stone.

Unlike the mother oyster who can do nothing for her eggs after she releases them, animals in other situations can help in all kinds of ways. They can produce bigger, tougher eggs that are less vulnerable to predators, they can guard the eggs, incubate them, feed the young, defend them from predators or teach them how to hunt. But the more the parents help their offspring, the fewer they can help. Every species balances the advantages of mass production against the benefits that come from spending time and effort supporting their young.

▼ Very few fish are fertilized internally, but the swordtail is one. Instead of producing a large number of eggs, the female produces only a few – and she nurtures them inside her body. When they are born the young fish are still very vulnerable, but their chances of survival are very much improved.

Caring Parents

▶ A baby chimpanzee is fed, protected and cared for by its mother, often with help from her female relatives. With this caring start in life the young chimp soon learns how to survive, and how to fit into chimpanzee society.

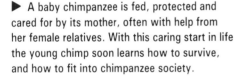

▶ ▶ This female dragonfly will never even see her offspring, but she does all she can to help them survive by taking great care to place her eggs in the safest possible place.

When animals first crawled out of the sea and onto the land millions of years ago, they had to face many new problems. They could float in the sea, but they had to stand on land. They were permanently wet in the sea, but they had to develop waterproof skins so that they would not dry out on land. And they had to change to breathing air. Just as important to their survival on land were the changes these early land animals had to make to their methods of reproduction.

In the sea it is possible for reproduction to be very simple. Eggs and sperm can just be released by the parents, and the sperm swim through the water to fertilize the eggs. But on land the eggs and sperm would dry up and die in seconds, so they had to be protected. Some animals that spend almost their entire lives on land have never really solved this problem, and return at breeding time to a pond or lake, or to the sea. Most frogs and toads are drawn back to water to complete this crucial stage in their life-cycle, and so are tropical land-crabs.

Only animals that live in very damp environments or have developed some form of internal fertilization can spend their entire lives on land. Internal fertilization makes it possible for many land animals to get eggs and sperm together safely, but it has other advantages, which is why it has also evolved in some sea creatures. When the eggs are fertilized inside the female she can do much more towards looking after her young.

▲ Most kinds of fly lay large numbers of eggs, but the female tsetse fly produces just one egg at a time, and after it is fertilized she retains it inside her body until it completes its development and hatches into a larva. She then gives birth, "laying" the larva on the ground where it pupates before finally emerging as winged adult.

One simple way in which a female can protect her fertilized egg is by covering it in a shell, which helps to prevent the developing embryo from drying out. This increases the time that eggs can survive on land, but no shell is completely watertight. All eggshells have tiny holes in them called "pores" which allow air to pass through so that the young animal growing inside can breathe. If the shell were airtight, the embryo would die from lack of oxygen.

Eggshells can even protect their contents from egg-eaters. The embryo growing inside the egg cannot search for food itself, and must be wrapped in its shell with enough food to last until its development is completed. This, of course, makes eggs particularly good food for any animal that finds them. The shell, however, provides a high degree of protection. It will keep out fungi and bacteria as well as a host of flies and beetles, while ostrich eggs are so tough that even lions cannot easily break them. Birds with smaller eggs rely on camouflage markings to hide them from large predators.

Even better protection is provided by those animals that do not lay their eggs but allow them to continue developing inside the body of the female. Insects, reptiles, amphibians and fishes can all provide examples of animals that have mastered this trick, which is called

ovoviviparity. At its simplest, in animals like the slow worm, the eggs remain inside the mother throughout their development, and hatch at the moment they are laid. Although the vast majority of insects lay eggs, the tsetse fly and the aphids are among the few that give birth to live young. The egg of the female tsetse fly actually hatches inside her, and she provides the growing larva with food from a special gland until she is ready to give birth.

Giving birth to live young allows females to protect their offspring through the first difficult days of life, and allows them to be born well developed and able to fend for themselves almost immediately. But carrying the young inside the body does have its disadvantages too. The extra weight slows the female, making her more likely to fall victim to predators herself. A duck that kept all her eggs inside her until they were fully developed would be unable to get off the ground for several weeks. This is probably why birds, which are so advanced in other ways, all retain the egg-laying habit, even though many of them continue to look after their young long after the eggs have hatched. In all these different ways, internal fertilization has led to parents giving a great deal more care to their offspring, but it also means that they can produce fewer of them.

▲ Young scorpions would make a tasty snack for many a desert bird, but carried on their mother's back and protected by her poisonous sting they are relatively safe from harm.

Should You Put All Your Eggs in One Basket?

On a warm day in summer white butterflies are a common sight, fluttering across fields and along hedgerows. Their flight is interrupted only briefly as they rest for a moment on a leaf, and then take off again. Eventually one will settle for longer, and then crawl beneath the leaf where she will carefully lay a whole batch of eggs. Usually the leaf she chooses is a cabbage leaf, which she has selected from all other leaves by tasting it with sensory organs on the tips of her legs. What she tastes is the mustard oil in the cabbage, and it is this taste for cabbage that gives the butterfly its common name — the cabbage white.

The female cabbage white is most particular about where she lays her eggs because the mustard oil in the leaves is essential to the survival of her young. As they hatch, the caterpillars start to eat the leaf they are on, and soon they grow into a conspicuous gang that quickly turns the leaf to lace. They do not even try to hide. Along with the cabbage leaves they eat the mustard oil which guided their mother to their food-plant, but instead of digesting it, they store it. Concentrated mustard oil tastes revolting — and after eating one cabbage white caterpillar, very few predators come back for more.

Although it is not immediately obvious, the female cabbage white butterfly looks after her young in two ways. She chooses the right plant to lay her eggs on, and she lays them in big clumps so that although a few may be eaten, most of them will survive. Even though she is probably miles away when her eggs hatch, she has already done all she can to ensure the survival of her young.

Other insects help their larvae in very different ways. Heliconids are large and beautiful butterflies from Central and South America, and their caterpillars eat the leaves of passion-flower plants. These leaves do not contain mustard oil or any other chemical that would make the caterpillar taste nasty, so a large group of caterpillars on a passion-flower would just represent a large and lucky find for a hunting bird.

As a result, heliconid butterflies do not lay all their eggs in a massive batch. Instead, they lay them singly, and they have developed a very elegant way for a female to make sure that there are not too many other caterpillars around where she lays an egg. Sticking out of the stem of the passion-flower are thin tendrils that help the plant to climb, and the butterfly will lay its single egg only on the tip of one of these tendrils. There is no room for a second egg on the tip, so there can never be a cluster of caterpillars. Taking that much care with each egg means that the female cannot produce as many eggs as the cabbage white, but at least they are unlikely to suffer as they would if she laid them carelessly.

A potter wasp goes even further than the heliconid in helping her larvae. The female collects mud and builds a small clay pot by carefully sticking mud balls together and shaping them with her jaws and feet. In the pot her egg would be safe, but it would starve, so the mother also supplies it with food. She catches caterpillars or spiders, paralyses them with her sting, and puts them into the clay egg-chamber. Then she lays her egg, hung on a thin thread from the roof of the pot so that the wriggling caterpillars cannot damage it. When she finally seals up the pot the egg inside is protected and the larva that hatches from it is guaranteed a good supply of food. The female then goes on to repeat the whole performance.

Insects will go to remarkable lengths to ensure that their eggs are laid in a place that gives their young the best chance of surviving. There are even parasitic flies that lay eggs on wasps and bees while their victims are flying. The larvae that hatch from these eggs have an excellent start in life because they are actually stuck onto their food, but not surprisingly the flies do not lay many eggs during their lifetime. As always, the more care an animal takes over where it places each egg, the fewer eggs it can lay.

▲ The eggs of this South American relative of the common cabbage white butterfly are all laid together and will all hatch at the same time.

Metamorphosis: the Miraculous Change

A caterpillar has to change completely before it can turn into a butterfly and take to the air. For days, weeks or even months it has to give up feeding and just sit there as a pupa while it undergoes the extraordinary process known as metamorphosis (literally "change of shape"). Inside the pupa, virtually the whole animal becomes like soup, and from this soup an adult butterfly eventually emerges. But while it is a pupa it can do nothing active to grow, reproduce or protect itself. Metamorphosis is a desperately complicated and risky process, so it must have enormous advantages to make it worthwhile. So what are the advantages of metamorphosis?

For a start, metamorphosis makes it possible for the young animal to live in a totally different way from the adult. One stage in the animal's life can be devoted to growing, without having to move much. The other stage can be highly mobile but without any need to grow very much. Because of the enormous changes that occur at metamorphosis, the two stages can specialize in very different roles and lifestyles.

This has several important consequences. A caterpillar and a butterfly eat totally different types of food. A caterpillar feeding on leaves can grow slowly and steadily throughout the spring, long before there are enough flowers to supply the nectar on which the adult butterflies will feed. Leaves are a plentiful and reliable source of food, but they are difficult to digest. Growing is the caterpillar's job, and leaves are the perfect food for that. During metamorphosis, it loses its leaf-cutting jaws and emerges as a butterfly equipped with a long tube called the proboscis, with which it will sip nectar from flowers. Nectar is a mixture of water and easily-digested sugars – the perfect high-energy fuel for powering flight, so the adult butterfly can fly about, court and mate. These are all tasks that the slow, lumbering caterpillar could never attempt.

Among insects it is usually the larvae that stay put and the adults that fly in search of new places to lay their eggs, but for many sea creatures the change goes the other way. Sea water is full of tiny animals swimming about, and a lot of these are larvae. Adult mussels and barnacles are permanently attached to rocks. Crabs, starfish and cockles can all move about to some extent but they do not usually move very far as adults. They all produce larvae that either swim or simply drift about in the sea-currents. Then the larvae change and settle down to colonize new areas and grow into adults.

Butterflies and moths spend their entire lives on land or in the air. Cockles and starfishes never leave the sea. But in some species metamorphosis is so dramatic that the animals can spend part of their lives in water and the rest on land. Such a transformation requires a complete change in the way the animals move, breathe and feed, but it does have additional benefits. Dragonflies fly about at high speed during the summer, but they die when winter comes. Their larvae survive the cold weather because they live at the bottom of ponds,

and although the surface waters may become frozen solid, the water lower down never freezes.

What young animals have to do is survive and grow. Creatures that go through metamorphosis can apply themselves totally to these tasks while they are young. They then change by metamorphosis into the adult which is devoted to the very different task of reproduction. By specializing in this way, both adults and young can perform their separate tasks more successfully.

▲ The nymph of this dragonfly spent two years on the bed of a stream, living on tadpoles, worms, insects and other small animals. After several intermediate stages it has now left the water and is emerging as a winged adult – one of the most beautiful and spectacular of all insect predators.

▲ The eggs of the North American monarch butterfly are laid on milkweed plants, which are the caterpillars' preferred food.

▼ Hatching monarch butterfly caterpillars eat their way out of their shells. (Some insect larvae cut their way free with sharp spines while the larvae of other species dissolve the shell wall with chemicals.)

▲ As it feeds on milkweed leaves the monarch caterpillar stores the plant's poisons in its body, and these act as a deterrent to predators.

▼ When it has reached full size, the monarch butterfly caterpillar enters the pupal stage suspended beneath a leaf.

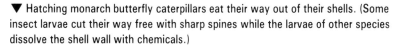

▶▶ Adult monarch butterflies are brightly coloured and this provides a warning to predators that their flesh is poisonous.

Caring Frogs and Midwife Toads

In Europe and North America there are relatively few different kinds of frogs and toads. Elsewhere, particularly in the tropics, there are hundreds of different species, with many strange lifestyles. In particular, they differ in how much the parents look after their young. In Britain, for example, the common frog simply lays a mass of spawn in a small pond and then both parents immediately abandon the eggs, leaving them to take their chances. The eggs' only protection is the mass of slimy jelly that surrounds them and makes them a slippery and difficult mouthful for ducks and fishes. At the other extreme is a small frog from Puerto Rico. Its eggs are fertilized while they are still inside the female's body, and four weeks after mating she gives birth to a batch of froglets.

▲ Red-eyed leaf frogs lay their eggs on damp leaves hanging over water in the warm, moist rainforests of South America. Hidden among the wet foliage the tadpoles are not completely safe, but here there are far fewer predators than there are in the forest stream below.

Between these two extremes lies a whole range of patterns of parental care. Frogs living in fast-flowing streams either attach their eggs to rocks and stones, or move into quiet backwaters in order to spawn. Some species make nests of foam for their eggs, others lay them in bowl-shaped nests scraped out of the mud by the male. Some frogs make nests of folded leaves in trees near the water, and in one species the nest is guarded by the female until the eggs hatch, when she helps the emerging tadpoles on their way by kicking them into the water

below! There are toads that carry their eggs on their backs, or in a long string looped around the legs of the male. Female poison-arrow frogs lay their eggs on land, and the male guards them until they hatch and then carries the tadpoles to water. The male Darwin's frog stays with the eggs once they have been laid, and when the tadpoles begin to move about inside them he picks them up and carries them about in his mouth for three weeks.

What is it that decides how much care a frog will take in looking

▲ In most poison-arrow frogs of South America, the males carry the tadpoles around on their backs until they are ready to change into frogs. (Frogs in this group have very toxic chemicals in their skin, and these are used by forest hunters to poison the tips of arrows and blowgun darts.)

after its young? If there are egg-eating predators in the local pond, then of course it makes sense to try and lay the eggs elsewhere, and small puddles or foam nests may provide a more secure site in which the young tadpoles can begin their development. This limits the number of eggs that the frog can produce, but it can be more successful when there are predators about. Exactly which method any particular frog species uses will depend on the climate, the numbers and types of predators on land and in the water, the sorts of nesting sites that are available, and even the sort of food that it eats.

We tend to think of simple animals as careless parents and more complex ones as taking increasingly greater care of their eggs. The frogs demonstrate quite clearly that even within a single group of animals, different species can adopt a wide range of different lifestyles. It is often difficult to understand why a particular animal has adopted one level of parental care rather than another because the balance between possible advantages and disadvantages is so complicated.

▲ The marsupial frog takes its name from the fact that it carries its offspring under a flap of skin on its back. The young eventually emerge as tadpoles, and the female uses the toes of her back feet to scoop them out of the pouch and into a suitable pool of water.

◀◀ Female common toads lay their eggs (spawn) in long strings of protective jelly which are wrapped around the stems of water plants.

Birds and Their Young

▶ A snow plover keeps a careful watch over its beautifully camouflaged eggs.

If human beings had invented the eggshell, the team responsible would have won a design award. An eggshell must be strong enough for the adult bird to sit on it, but fragile enough for the chick to be able to chip its way out. It must be porous, so that air can seep through to provide the chick inside with oxygen. At the same time, it must provide a seal so that not too much water evaporates from the egg during the time it is being incubated. The eggshell is a wonderful life-support capsule for the developing chick – so good, in fact, that all birds' eggs are virtually the same.

The eggs of different species of bird may all be very similar, but the parents look after them in very different ways. At one extreme, the female malee fowl lays up to 35 eggs, and although these eggs are carefully looked after, the young birds get no help at all from either parent once they hatch. At the other extreme are the king penguins.

▶ The panel at the right shows the development of a bird from fertilization of the egg to hatching. The upper line of illustrations shows the size of the embryo in relation to the egg: the lower line of illustrations shows in more detail the development of the chick at roughly the same times.

It takes about 21 days for the chick to develop. To begin with it looks like a tiny exclamation mark on top of the yolk, and as it grows, blood vessels spread out to cover the yolk which contains its food supply. At this stage the embryo looks like a tiny tadpole, but soon the limbs appear and by about ten days old it is recognizable as a bird. For the next ten days it continues to grow until it is big enough to survive outside the safety of its shell.

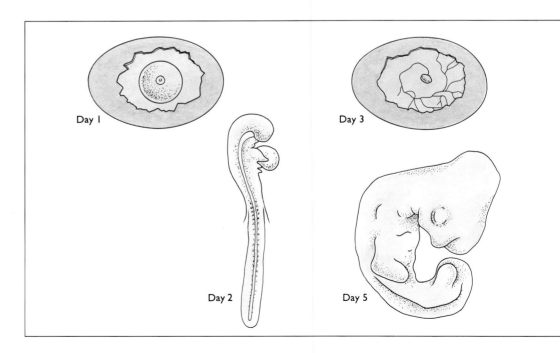

Day 1

Day 2

Day 3

Day 5

Their single egg is laid in December and the parents take turns to incubate it for the next eight weeks, in temperatures that are always well below freezing. Then, when the chick hatches, they continue to feed it for a further ten months, until the start of the next summer.

The reason for the difference between the "careless" malee fowl and the "careful" penguin lies in the way the two species live. Penguins must catch their food in the sea, so there is absolutely no way that the chick can feed itself before it can even swim. The parents simply have to feed it, but they can only look after one chick at a time, so they take great care of it. Malee fowl feed chiefly on seeds and insects, and there is no way that the parents could find and carry enough food for their chicks. The different situations of the two types of bird make them breed in very different ways, even if the eggs they lay look similar on the surface.

▲ Emperor penguins keep their eggs, and later their chicks, balanced on the tops of their feet where they are covered by the loose skin of the lower part of the parent's body. This way the egg or chick is kept safe and warm – a perfect adaption to the bitter cold of the emperor's Antarctic breeding grounds.

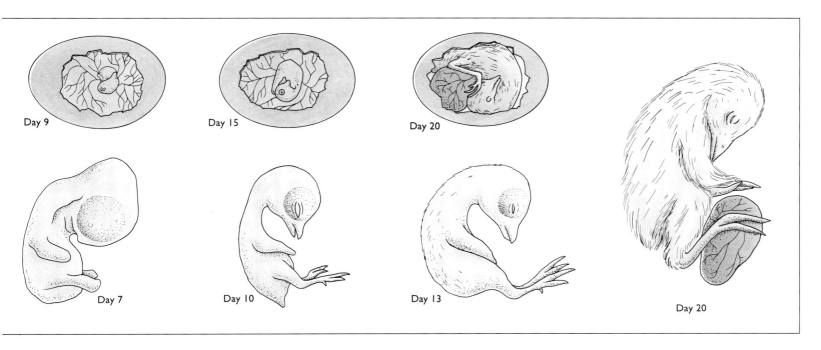

Day 9

Day 15

Day 20

Day 7

Day 10

Day 13

Day 20

The Mammals

Before the discovery of South America and Australia, the only mammals know to Western scientists were the placental mammals. These all produce their young in much the same way. The egg develops in the ovary and is fertilized inside the mother's body where it begins to develop. The egg divides several times, and the embryo then attaches itself to the wall of the mother's womb. The wall of the womb then thickens and develops a rich supply of blood vessels. Food and oxygen flowing in these blood vessels are absorbed by the placenta, which is the life-support system for the developing young. This ingenious system is the most comprehensive form of parental care adopted by any group of animal, but not all mammals protect and nourish their young in the same way.

▲ One of the main characteristics of mammals is that they all feed their young on milk produced by special glands (mammary glands) on the chest or abdomen of the female. This baby olive baboon is being fed in virtually the same way as an infant dolphin, bat, human, seal, mouse or bear would be.

In the streams and ponds of Australia there lives one of the strangest creatures on Earth. When the first skins of the duck-billed platypus were sent back to England, scientists were very cautious. They feared that perhaps this weird new discovery was a hoax, a duck's beak sewn onto the body of some unknown mammal. We now know that the platypus is one of the last remaining representatives of an ancient group of mammals called monotremes. The monotremes are definitely mammals because they have a thick coat of fur, they are warm-blooded, and they feed their young on milk. What makes them so peculiar is that unlike all other mammals, the monotremes lay eggs.

Like reptile eggs, the eggs of the platypus are soft-shelled. They hatch after only ten days and the young stay with their mother for between three and four months, but although they feed on milk, the mother does not have teats. Instead, the young suck the milk from the fur around the openings of her mammary glands.

The eggs of the platypus are laid in a burrow, but the eggs of the other living monotreme, the echidna or spiny anteater, are laid in a pouch on the mother's abdomen. Here they remain for ten days before hatching, and the young remain inside the pouch until their spines begin to appear. Like the female platypus, the mother echidna has no teats and the young suck milk that oozes from the mammary glands and soaks into the mother's fur.

◀ Most small placental mammals produce several litters during the breeding season, and this pattern is also found in many of the small marsupials such as this fat-tailed dunnart which inhabits the dry regions of southern Australia. This tiny insect-eating marsupial usually produces young twice a year, between the middle of winter (July) and the summer months of January-February. The young are first suckled in the mother's pouch, and then for a further 60 days in a grass-lined nest in a hollow log or under a large rock.

In addition to the placental mammals and the monotremes, there is a third group of mammals, the marsupials, which includes the kangaroos, wombats, koalas and opossums. Marsupial eggs are like those of monotremes, but these eggs are never actually laid. Instead, the tiny young are born while still very poorly developed. The young of the largest kangaroos, for example, weigh only about three-hundredths of an ounce (1 gram) at birth — about the same as an aspirin tablet. When the young kangaroo is born it crawls through the fur on the mother's belly and into a deep pouch on her abdomen. There it attaches itself firmly to one of the teats, and remains there, feeding, while it continues its development. Marsupials have teats very similar to those of the placental mammals. The pouch is virtually a second womb for the baby kangaroo, and there it enjoys protection until it is fully developed and able to feed and travel on its own.

After birth, young mammals are provided with ideal food in the form of their mothers' milk, and they are protected from predators and other dangers by the mother and sometimes by the father as well. Mammals make an enormous effort to look after their young, and consequently they can only look after a few at a time. But by taking such care of their young, mammals have become some of the most successful land animals ever to have evolved on Earth.

▶ An eastern grey kangaroo and "joey" drying out after an all-night storm. Marsupials use a system of infant care that is very different from that of the placental mammals. The young are born when only a few millimetres long and not even completely developed. They then transfer to the mother's pouch where they complete their development in a warm, safe environment. A young joey will continue to spend time in the pouch long after it has stopped suckling and started to feed itself.

FAMILY LIFE

Many animal mothers protect their offspring during the early stages while the embryo develops, and this is most obvious in the womb of a mammal or the shell of an egg. But eventually this protection becomes a prison, and sooner or later the time comes when the young must emerge into the world and begin the next stage of their journey towards independence.

The first few days of a young animal's life are by far the most dangerous. Even when it can do some things for itself it is still very small and vulnerable, and easy prey for predators who are always on the look-out for an easy meal. Yet despite the dangers many of the young do survive, and this is often due largely to the continuing protection provided by their parents.

▶ These beautiful Australian black swans show the high level of parental care provided by many of the larger waterbirds. Both parents share the task of guarding the cygnets, and will not hesitate to attack if a predator comes anywhere near them.

Hatching and Birth

▶ Like most birds, the silver pheasant chick must chip its way out of its shell without any help from its parents. In large clutches like those of pheasants and other gamebirds, the chicks communicate before they hatch, using soft chirping calls. This helps them coordinate their hatching efforts so that they all break out at the same time.

At first the air that seeps through the shell of a bird's egg is more than enough to meet the needs of the tiny chick growing inside, but as the chick reaches its full size it begins to suffocate. Carbon dioxide builds up inside the shell, and this acts as a trigger which stimulates the chick to absorb the last remains of its yolk sac and begin the movements that will eventually release it from its cage. A powerful "hatching muscle" on the back of the chick's neck begins to twitch, driving its beak against the shell. The beak of a young chick is reinforced with a horny egg-tooth, which helps it to chip the first all-important hole through the shell. Once a hole is made, the chick can breathe fresh air. It then rests, sometimes for days, before beginning the next phase of its journey. Then the hatching movements begin again, and after each hole is made in the shell the chick pushes with its right foot, twisting itself slightly inside the shell so that its next attack lands on a new spot. Eventually the chick cuts right round the shell, or at least far enough to be able to push out a large section, and struggles out through the hole.

Birds with large cluches of eggs take many days to lay them all, and this creates problems, particularly for birds like the grouse. Almost immediately after the eggs hatch, the mother leads her young away from the nest, with the result that chicks run the risk of being left behind if they hatch later than their brothers and sisters. The mother helps to synchronize their hatching by waiting until her last egg is laid before beginning to incubate the clutch, but it is the chicks themselves that decide exactly when they will emerge. When they are about to hatch, the chicks call to each other by making a quiet clicking sound. Somehow this hurries those chicks that have yet to start breaking through the shell, and even more remarkably the rest of the chicks seem to wait until the whole clutch is ready. Then they all hatch at the same time, often within the space of a couple of hours.

Like birds, some reptiles have an egg-tooth which they use to cut their way out of their shells. In crocodiles and turtles this is a horny lump similar to the egg-tooth on the beak of a bird, but snakes grow a real tooth in the centre of the upper lip and they use this to slash their way out of the shell by driving the head from side to side. Fish and frogs, on the other hand, do not cut their way free; instead they secrete special chemicals which digest the thin membranes which surround them.

Monotremes face similar problems to birds and reptiles when emerging into the world, and like birds they have an egg-tooth which is used to cut a hole in the shell. However, the young of most placental mammals face very different problems. The barrier between themselves and the outside world is not so much the membranes that surround them but their mother's birth canal.

In mammals, as in all other animals, it is the young that decide on the right time to emerge. When it has reached maturity in the womb, the foetus begins to produce chemicals that cause changes in the placenta and the wall of the mother's womb. The placenta and womb respond by producing their own chemicals, which eventually cause the muscles of the womb to begin contracting. During labour the contractions of the muscles surrounding the womb force the foetus down the birth canal and out into the world.

▼ When they are born, baby wood mice are blind, hairless and totally dependent on their mother. Within a week their hair will grow and their eyes will open, but they will rely for some time on the mother's protection and on the safety of the warm, grass-lined nest in its underground burrow.

The Young Ones

For many animals the task of looking after the young does not end with birth or hatching. Although insects, amphibians and reptiles often never see their eggs again once they have been laid, most birds and all mammals continue to look after their young long after they first open their eyes on the world. The womb and the eggshell provide protection through the first weeks or months of life, but newborn and newly hatched young are still very vulnerable, so parents often have to provide protection for many more weeks or even months.

There are many ways in which parents can look after their offspring. The young must eat, and the nature of their food often determines how the parents can help them. Young ducks and gamebirds leave the nest almost immediately after hatching, but for the first few weeks they usually stay close to their mother who helps them to find suitable food. The food of seabirds is more difficult to catch, and so the young spend longer in the nest and their food is brought to them by their parents until they are old enough to fly and forage for themselves. Hawks and falcons usually feed on birds and small mammals. These are not only difficult to catch but in addition the parents must tear the food into small pieces before it can be swallowed by small chicks. In large birds of prey it is common for the young to remain with their parents for several months before they are able to hunt and feed by themselves.

▶ A female kestrel feeds her chicks in the nest for many weeks after they hatch. The death of the mouse was sudden and dramatic as the kestrel plunged from its hovering flight with talons and bill outstretched for the kill. But when she is at the nest the female is almost dainty in her actions as she tears strips of meat from the body and presents them to her chicks.

◀ Many young birds produce their droppings in neat white packages called faecal sacs. By removing these from the nest, this song thrush will prevent the growth of bacteria that might be harmful to her chicks.

As well as providing food, birds and mammals look after their young in other less obvious ways. Many different species of bird help to keep their nests clean by removing the waste that the chicks produce. Waste is produced by the chicks in neat little packages called faecal sacs, and after a feeding trip the adults collect these sacs in their beaks and either drop them well away from the nest or swallow them. This helps to keep the nest free of parasites and disease. Mammals that give birth in nests perform much the same service by licking and grooming their nursing young, stimulating them to excrete and cleaning up the waste at the same time. Because the young only excrete in response to this grooming, the nest or den never becomes dirty.

◀ This white-tailed deer is licking her fawn to stimulate it to empty its bowels. For the first few weeks of its life the fawn remains hidden, except for the brief periods when the mother returns to suckle it. During this time, the fawn excretes only in response to the mother's grooming, and this ensures that the youngster leaves fewer tell-tale scent clues that could disclose its hiding place to predators.

▲ Painted storks live in southern Asia where temperatures are always high. Looking after young storks involves not only feeding them but also bringing them water and shading them from the intense heat of the Sun.

Nidicolous chicks hatch naked and unable to walk

Nidifugous (precocial) chicks are down-covered at hatching

Many young birds and mammals arrive in the world naked. Without the insulation of fur or feathers they rely on their parents to regulate their body temperature. If the parents die, it is often extreme heat or cold that kills the young, rather than a lack of food. Young guinea pigs, for example, can eat solid food as soon as they are born and so they can survive without their mother's milk, but in the wild a deserted litter would not survive a single cold night.

Birds and mammals also help their young by protecting them against predators. Many animals produce alarm calls in the face of danger, and the young respond to these calls by remaining still and quiet so as not to attract attention. An alarm call also helps by drawing the attention of a predator to the animal that made the call. This puts the parents at some risk themselves, but adult birds and mammals are far more likely to survive an attack than their helpless young. If the alarm call fails, the parents may try to drive the predator away from the nest. Birds will attack snakes and lizards much bigger than themselves, and the first lesson for any tourist venturing into the great game reserves of Africa is that there is nothing in nature more dangerous than a mother protecting her young.

Distraction displays and alarm calls

▲ A stone curlew feigning injury to lure an intruder away from the nest.

Animals that have no weapons use other types of defence when a predator threatens their young. Stone curlews and many other ground-nesting birds put on a very complicated performance when they spot a predator approaching. First the mother creeps silently away from the nest, leaving her eggs or chicks. Then she flies around calling loudly, making diving attacks on the predator. Finally she may land on the ground nearby and begin limping around, dragging one wing behind her. By playing the part of a wounded bird she lures the predator away from her chicks, hoping to rely on her speed and flying skill to escape from its final charge or pounce.

These displays certainly work on humans, so they probably have some success distracting other predators. But in the long term one of the most successful parts of the whole performance may well be the alarm calls that the mother makes. For one thing the alarm calls often attract other birds which all start calling and "mobbing" the predator. This in itself can often make the predator retreat because at this point there is clearly no longer any chance at all of making a surprise attack.

Alarm calls have an immediate effect on the chicks. As soon as they hear their mother's call, they freeze and crouch down. They also learn to identify the object that their mother has been alarmed by, and mobbing behaviour may well do the same thing by helping the young learn what predators look like. Birds nesting in a field of cows do not make alarm calls at the cows, but they do at humans, dogs or foxes. The chicks learn which animals to look out for, and this can easily save their lives as they grow.

It is dangerous for the stone curlew to defend her chicks, and teach them what to beware of, but it is a vital part of ensuring their survival. The mother's reproductive success depends on the survival of those young, so she simply *has* to teach them about predators.

Mother in Charge

▶ This one-day-old Asian elephant calf may remain with its mother for the next ten years, but is very unlikely ever to meet its father.

Whether it is cows with their calves, ewes with their lambs or a she-bear with her cubs, it is almost always the mother we see with her young. We rarely stop to ask why it is usually the female and not the male that does most of the parental chores. The burden so often falls on the mother that nature seems to be sexist. In fact there is a very simple reason why, in so many animals, it is the female who does most of the work. She is the one with most to gain by it.

The female takes on the work of looking after the young because she produces only a relatively small number of eggs. Often the best way for her to have more surviving young is to look after them. For males things are different. They produce billions of sperm, and in theory one male can be the father of billions of offspring – far more than any one female can produce. So the best way for a male to have more young is usually to mate with as many females as possible. Hanging around to look after the young once they are born would only interfere with his efforts to find more females to mate with. This fundamental difference between males and females both forces the mother to take on the job of parental care and forces males to advertise for mates.

Among land animals there is a second reason why the mother is the one that generally looks after the young. Animals that breed on land have to protect their eggs and sperm from drying out, and the most common and most successful way to do this is for the adults to mate. That way, the eggs can be fertilized safely inside the mother's body. After mating, the embryos are retained inside the mother's body so she is bound to look after them, at least for the short time it takes to lay her eggs. So internal fertilization leaves the mother stuck with looking after the young.

The animal group in which the mother does most is the mammals. Mammal offspring start life inside the mother's womb, where they are

protected and fed during the gestation period. Pregnancy helps the offspring enormously, but it means that the mother can only produce a very small number of young. During pregnancy the mother puts a great deal of energy and effort into producing her young and she carries on doing so after they are born.

The chief way that mammals care for their new-born young is, of course, by feeding them with milk. Mother's milk gives an excellent start in life because it is a rich and nutritious food. It also contains proteins called antibodies that help the young to fight infection and disease. (This is one reason why breast-feeding is so good for human babies, especially in the first few weeks of life.)

A mammal mother can do a great deal for her offspring, and most male mammals can do very little to help her. When they are first born, a male's offspring drink only their mother's milk. Even when they are weaned, the father can do little to help feed them. The vast majority of mammals are vegetarian and feed on grass, leaves or seeds, and even young animals quickly learn to find these foods just as efficiently as their parents. When the father can do nothing to help his offspring, he gains nothing from being with them. The best way for such a male to try and increase the number of offspring he produces is to leave his young in the care of their mother and set about trying to mate with other females.

We think of it as natural for mothers to be the caring parents largely because the animals most familiar to us are mammals, and young mammals are dependent on their mother's milk. For other animals – birds, reptiles, amphibians, fishes and insects – there is no reason at all why the father cannot look after the young just as well as the mother. And although male mammals cannot produce milk, there are other ways in which they can help.

▲ Here, a female long-eared bat feeds her twin young from nipples high on her body, under her wings. Suckling gives the young a very good start in life but it does mean that in mammals it is the female that usually takes the chief role as parent. The young of most of the smaller bats develop quickly and fly at about three weeks old. In larger species such as the tropical fruit bats, it may take up to three months.

Sharing Parenthood

▶ Many parental tasks can be carried out equally well by the mother or the father, and in the case of the common tern both parents will repeatedly "dive-bomb" an approaching predator or birdwatcher to drive the threat away from the nest.

Pheasants and kingfishers are both common and successful groups of birds, but their approach to family life could hardly be more different. Pheasant chicks feed on seeds and the occasional insect, and are able to feed themselves almost as soon as they hatch. They do not need to be fed by their parents, so a male pheasant can do very little to help them survive. During the spring and summer there is no shortage of food. Even when she is incubating, the hen can leave the nest, quickly eat her fill, and return to the nest while the eggs are still warm, so the male does not even need to take his turn at sitting. Instead, he concentrates his efforts on defending his territory and attracting as many females as possible. For the male kingfisher this carefree lifestyle would be a disaster. There is a great deal that he can do to help his chicks, and if he does not do his share, very few of his offspring will survive.

The male kingfisher's work starts even before he mates with his partner. Fish are always hard to catch, and the female needs all the food she can get. The better she feeds while she is forming the eggs, the more eggs she will be able to lay, and this is one reason why the male feeds her as part of their courtship. It is partly ritual, partly a test of his fishing ability, and partly a way for him to increase the brood size, and so increase the number of his offspring.

As well as feeding his mate, the male kingfisher helps her to dig their nest-hole, and by the time the eggs are laid, the male has worked almost as hard for them as the female. But this is just the beginning. He will also help her to incubate the clutch, and to feed the chicks when they hatch. This feeding is the biggest job, and both parents have to join in if they are to raise a reasonable-sized brood.

Nine out of every ten bird species have a family structure like that

▲ Catching fish for a hungry brood of kingfisher chicks is an exhausting job. Each of the 6–7 chicks will eat up to 15 fish a day, so each parent must catch at least 50 fish every day – in addition to catching food for themselves!

▲ A human father can do everything for his baby except breast-feed it, but just how involved a father is with his new-born child varies greatly from one society to another and from one individual to another.

▶▶ From the moment a litter of fox cubs is weaned, the father can play an important part in feeding them. One successful hunt will bring home a rabbit or a large bird such as a chicken or pheasant, and this will provide the family's food needs for the day.

of the kingfisher, in which both mother and father work together to raise the young. So why is it that male birds help so often and male mammals so rarely? Part of the answer is that male birds help because they can. Birds feed their young on food that can be collected by either parent, and in the same way either parent can take on the work of brooding, nest building and protection. If the male can help, he usually does because in this way he is likely to raise more young than if he embarks on the rather uncertain course of chasing after more females. This is as true for mammals as for birds, and in the few cases where male mammals can help the female to raise her young they often do.

One mammal in which the male helps to raise the cubs is the red fox. The foxes' breeding season starts in the middle of winter when their unearthly screams often split the night and terrorize anybody who is awake. This horror used to be restricted to the countryside, but now many town-dwellers suffer (or enjoy) it as well.

Later, in about March, the vixen produces her litter, and both parents set about rearing the cubs. For several weeks the vixen stays close to the den and the dog fox brings back food. He is well able to help in this way because the food that the cubs eat is relatively easy for him to carry. A chicken stolen from a hen run will keep the cubs alive for a whole day, but it would need great armfuls of grass or hay to keep a family of herbivores fed.

Providing food is not the only way that a male mammal can improve the chances that his young will survive. The nocturnal owl monkeys of South America are almost entirely vegetarian, and the males do next to nothing towards feeding their young. Nevertheless, the female is almost incapable of raising an infant on her own because quite soon after they are born the young are too heavy for her to carry. Only by dividing the work between both parents can owl monkeys reproduce successfully. The male does most of the carrying, leaving the female free to conserve her energy and keep up her milk supply.

On the other hand there are many examples of males that *could* help with the chores of parenthood but never do. Leopards kill larger prey than foxes, and males could quite easily help supply the cubs with food, but they do not. There are several possible reasons for this sort of behaviour. First of all, evolution has selected individuals that do everything to make sure that they leave as many offspring as possible. If the father's lifestyle means that this is achieved by helping the mother raise the cubs, then he will help, but if it means that he does better by leaving the mother in order to search for other females, then he will leave. Male leopards have very large territories that may include the territories of several females. Since his partner can raise her cubs perfectly well without his help, there is no reason for him to stay with her and risk missing the chance to mate with another female.

Another reason why males ignore their young when they could help to look after them is that it is often difficult for a male to be sure that the young are his. A mother can always be certain that her offspring are really related to her, and that by looking after them she is passing on her genes. For the father things are much more complicated. There is always a chance that while his partner was receptive, another male might have mated with her as well. If he cannot be absolutely certain that he has fathered all the young in a litter, a male is more likely to desert the female and search for a new mate.

Nursemaid Fathers

We tend to think it natural for mothers to be the caring parents largely because, in mammals, the young are usually dependent on their mothers for quite some time. In other animal groups there is no obvious reason why the father cannot look after the young equally well, but still it is generally the mother that does the work. However, there are exceptions.

Traditional ideas about sex roles are turned on their head by animals like the stickleback. These are little fish that live in ponds and streams, and in their case it is the male that looks after the young and the female that abandons them. From the very start, the male does all the work. He builds a nest and then leads a female to it. There she lays her eggs, and immediately after she has done so the male swims over them, releasing his sperm to fertilize them. Meanwhile, the female swims off, and from then on the male looks after the eggs alone, fanning water over them, keeping them clean, and defending them against other small fish that might try to eat them.

▶ A male stickleback will care for his young from the moment the eggs are laid until the young fish are hatched and ready to fend for themselves. His red belly and blue eyes attract females to lay their eggs in his nest, and from then on he is in sole charge. He fertilizes them, protects them, fans clean water over them, and even when they hatch he remains on duty, chasing away predators for whom the fry would make a tasty meal.

Most fishes simply lay their eggs among weeds or scatter them to float free in the oceans. Parental care in fishes is the exception rather than the rule, but when fish do look after their young it is often the father, not the mother, who takes on the work. There are two reasons for this. First, most fishes fertilize their eggs externally and so the female must lay her eggs before the male fertilizes them. While he is spraying his sperm onto the eggs, the female can make a quick get-away, leaving him literally "holding the baby".

The deserted father has two options. He can either abandon the fertilized eggs and look for another female to mate with, or he can look after the eggs. Which should he do? The answer is simple, and is the second reason why it is so often the male fishes that look after their young. If he leaves, the stickleback will have wasted all the time and energy it took to build his nest and to court the female. But if he stays, he loses nothing. Other females may still come to lay in his nest – in fact female sticklebacks actually prefer to mate with males who are already guarding eggs because this means that they will spend more time protecting the young and less time courting new females.

For animals whose eggs are fertilized internally, the situation is rather different. When the female gives birth, the male may be miles away, and so it is usually the female that ends up looking after the young. The animals that are most familiar to us breed in this way, so we tend to think of female parental care as normal. The stickleback should make us question that, and among birds there are also exceptions to the general rule. When the female cannot raise her young on her own, the male is forced to stay and help look after them. This can go a step further. By doing all the work of looking after the young himself, the father can liberate the female to feed up so that she is soon in condition to mate with him again. Then, the male may do even better by allowing the female to abandon the young entirely to his care. When this happens, it is likely that the roles of male and female are totally reversed, with the female courting the male, and fighting with other females for territory. This total role reversal cannot happen in mammals because all young mammals must be fed on milk, and only females can produce milk.

▲ A male giant water bug carries on his back the clutch of eggs he fertilized.

▼ The male rhea of South America courts several females, which mate with him and lay eggs in his nest. He then incubates the eggs and cares for the young rheas.

Animal Aunts

Many young animals are totally helpless when they are born, and need looking after. Young chimpanzees will spend four or five years with their mothers. At first, they are entirely dependent on their mother's milk, but even when they begin to eat solid foods, young chimps cannot survive on their own. They need protection, and since they cannot keep up with the rest of the troop, they need to be carried. They must have the ticks and fleas picked out of their hair. Perhaps most important of all, they must learn how to fit into chimpanzee society – how to fight, and how to keep out of fights they might lose. They must learn how to make friends, because friends will be allies in times of trouble. The young chimp's mother does most of this work, but she often has help from other chimps – particularly her female relatives.

Female chimps mate with many different males, so the males cannot tell which babies are theirs. Consequently they show little interest in looking after any of them. Aunts are different. They carry some of the same genes as their nephews and nieces. A chimpanzee aunt can make sure that part of her survives into the future by helping to look after her sister's offspring. If she has not yet given birth herself, she also gets a chance to learn how to hold and look after a baby, and this practice will make her a better mother when her time comes. Having the aunts as helpers benefits the mother by easing her work-load, the young chimp by providing extra protectors and teachers, and the aunts by giving them valuable practice in parenthood.

◀ Two female Asian elephants keep a watchful eye on a baby as it enjoys a mud bath. This kind of shared responsibility is common in elephants. The natural mother is often helped by younger female relatives, and as they help they also benefit by learning some of the skills of being a parent.

◀ Like many members of the whale family, these bottle-nosed dolphins have a well-organized society in which the animals help each other. When a baby dolphin is born, the mother is usually accompanied by other females who will help her guide the infant to the surface for its first breath of air. The whole group will also cooperate to defend their young against attacks by predators.

Crèches

▶ An adult meerkat acts as baby-sitter for the young ones of the colony. These curious mongooses of the dry lands of southern Africa live in extended family bands in which all the animals are closely related. They have a complex social organisation in which all the adults take turns in minding the young while the rest of the pack is out hunting.

Without a crèche or a child-minder, human mothers find it very difficult to go out to work. Babies and toddlers make it almost impossible to concentrate on anything for very long, and whatever work the mother is trying to do is constantly interrupted by distractions. To leave the youngsters at home alone is impossible: there are just too many dangers.

Many birds face exactly the same dilemma. For some birds the answer is to make their nests so well hidden that the parents *can* take the risk of leaving their young unattended for short periods while they go off in search of food. But other birds must raise their young in areas where there is no cover and an unguarded nest would be left exposed to the eyes of watchful predators. In the icy wastes of Antarctica, there is not a single tree or bush in which to hide a nest, and the penguins that breed there have been forced to find some other way of protecting their young.

The solution adopted by the Antarctic penguins is to leave their chicks in crèches. These are unlike the crèches for human toddlers in that no adult is left permanently on guard, but there are usually a few adults dotted around the margins of a crèche, either feeding young chicks or resting. The presence of these birds, or perhaps just the sheer number of chicks massed closely together on the ice, helps to deter attacks by predators such as skuas. In some penguin species the crèches may become enormous gatherings with hundreds of birds, and as well as deterring predators the mass of bodies also helps the chicks to keep warm.

In the crèche, each bird is still fed only by its parents as they return from the sea every three or four days with a fresh load of food. In the

Arctic the chicks of eider ducks also form crèches. Eider ducklings, however, are not fed by their parents since they are quite capable of dabbling for scraps of food as soon as they reach the water. The crèches of eider ducks are also different in that they are guarded by older ducklings. As with penguins, one important advantage of being in a crèche is that the birds are less likely to fall victim to birds of prey. A single chick all on its own is far more likely to be killed by a skua than one that is a member of a large group.

It is rare to find animals that are prepared to spend much time or energy looking after young that are not their own, which is probably why crèches have evolved so rarely as a system of caring for the young. It is surprising, therefore, to find that in packs of dwarf mongooses, completely unrelated animals take turns in looking after the pack's young, and that these animals are often more dedicated baby-sitters than older relatives. Dwarf mongooses live in packs of 10 to 20 animals. Some of these will be related to each other while others will have joined the pack after being forced out of the pack they were born in. In a pack, only a single male and female breed each year, and the other pack members share the work of looking after the young. When the group goes off to search for food, one adult always stays behind to guard the den. Although the young that the baby-sitter guards are not its own, the time it spends caring for them will eventually be repaid. As the pack grows larger, there are more and more eyes to keep watch for hawks and falcons while the animals are out in the open, foraging for food. And eventually, if the baby-sitter reaches a dominant position in the pack, its turn to breed will come around and then the young it helped to raise will become baby-sitters themselves.

▲ In a king penguin crèche there may be several thousand young birds. Each chick is fed only by its own parents, but the whole group gains protection against predators by remaining huddled together in a dense mass.

Mother's Little Helpers

Watching a flock of bee-eaters swoop and dive as they catch insects on the wing, it is easy to overlook the most interesting thing about the biology of these beautiful birds. As they turn in the sky, flashing their yellow, blue and green plumage and chattering their soft, throaty calls, they put on a mesmerizing display. Only the careful bird-watcher who spends hours sitting beneath the high-rise complex of nest-holes in their sand-bank colonies is likely to notice anything unusual. What is peculiar about these birds is that at many of the nests more than two adults are helping to raise the chicks.

The bee-eaters form pairs to breed, and each pair builds a nest. The female lays the eggs, and both birds incubate them. Then, when they start to catch food and bring it to the chicks, the unexpected happens. Other birds arrive and start helping the parents, bringing food and feeding the chicks. These helpers are adult birds that are not breeding themselves.

It is unusual to find an animal not breeding when it has the opportunity. Males may fail to breed if they lose all their fights, and all animals have a period while they are growing to full maturity when they cannot breed, but all mature animals must try to breed if they are to pass on their genes to the next generation. So why do some perfectly healthy bee-eaters not only sacrifice the opportunity to breed themselves, but

◀ Carmine bee-eaters nest in large noisy colonies, in nest burrows dug in an earth bank. Some of the adults bringing food to the young are not actually parents, but young adults who are helping their older brothers and sisters to raise their families.

actually help others to raise their chicks instead?

In the case of the bee-eaters, there is an explanation. The helpers are not just any birds: they are close relatives of the breeding pair, usually brothers or sisters of one of the parents. What they are doing is helping their close relatives breed. Brothers and sisters do not have the same set of genes unless they are identical twins, but they do have very similar sets of genes. In fact, in genetic terms brothers and sisters are as closely related to each other as they are to their parents. By helping his brother or sister to breed, a bee-eater is not passing on his own genes to the next generation but he is doing the next best thing because he is helping to pass on a set of genes that is very similar to his own.

The birds being helped certainly benefit from having their brothers or sisters bring food to the nest, but the helpers may benefit as well. It is usually young birds that end up as helpers, and these inexperienced youngsters will inevitably have had problems finding a mate of their own. It is quite likely that while helping, a bird learns things that will make him or her a better parent the next year. So the helpers may be gaining directly from their actions by making their own future breeding more successful, and at the same time helping some of their own genes into the next generation. Helping is not as good as producing young, but for some animals at least, it is the next best thing.

Cuckoos: the Artful Nest-hijackers

Like most animals, a reed warbler suffers from parasites. There are tapeworms and roundworms that live inside it, and there are lice and fleas that live among (and even inside) its feathers. But these only attack its body, and generally they do only limited damage. The most disastrous parasite of the reed warbler is one that does not even touch it. Even so it steals one of a reed warbler's greatest assets – the way it looks after its offspring. This parasite is the cuckoo.

Reed warblers emerge into the world blind and helpless. Immediately the chicks hatch, the parents are there to protect and feed them. For several weeks they continue darting to and fro all day long catching insects. Having such caring parents is a great advantage to the chicks; they have a wonderful start in life, and only have to take on the challenge of fending for themselves once they are almost full grown. The cuckoo turns these model parents to her own advantage by laying her egg in the reed warbler's nest.

▶ Reed warblers are one of the main host species for the European cuckoo, and despite the huge difference in size between the two, the warbler ''foster-parents'' never reject the cuckoo chick. The inside of its mouth is the same colour as that of the reed warblers' own chicks, and the feeding instinct triggered by the bright orange gape is just too strong to resist.

As soon as it hatches, the baby cuckoo takes over. First it pushes all the reed warbler eggs and chicks out of the nest. Then it eats all the food that the parents can bring, and it grows fast, keeping them fully occupied. The sight of a chick with its beak open triggers the reed warblers' parental instincts and they work all day, cramming food into the ever-open mouth. Normally this is a successful part of their routine as caring parents, because open beaks in their nest should belong to their own chicks. But the cuckoo's deception is perfect. The inside of the cuckoo chick's beak is exactly the same colour as that of a reed warbler chick, and even the intruder's huge size and strange appearance do not interfere with the adults' feeding instincts.

Cuckoos depend on parental care as much as any other bird, but they cheat by tricking other birds such as reed warblers into providing that care. There are 127 different cuckoos around the world, and of these about 45 are nest parasites, each one specializing in tricking one or two regular host species.

Animals like cuckoos are known as brood parasites or nest parasites, and they are quite common. Birds suffer particularly from brood parasites because of the way in which they look after their offspring. Birds have to deposit their eggs in nests, and look after them there until the chicks are big enough to survive on their own. If the eggs are left unattended for even a minute, a brood parasite can slip in and lay her egg among the others while the parents' backs are turned. The more care the parents take of their young, the more attractive they are to a brood parasite.

Brood parasites exploit most animals that lay eggs and then look after their young, but the cuckoo is so much the best-known example that its name is often borrowed and used to describe these creatures generally. Cuckoo bees lay their eggs in the nests of bumble bees. When they hatch, they eat the eggs of the bumble bees and then grow on the food that their hosts bring. Parasites generally give people the creeps, but there is something both wonderful and horrible about the brood parasite's highly specialized way of life.

◀ The magpie builds its own nest in which to lay its eggs and raise its chicks. However, a female will sometimes also play the role of cuckoo by laying eggs in the nests of other magpies nearby. If she gets away with the trick, more of her genes will be carried into the next generation – and she will have done none of the work of feeding those extra mouths. Surface markings distinguish the eggs of different individuals, but unless the host bird actually see another magpie laying an egg in her nest there is little chance that she will notice and push it out.

Social

Insects

Most people are a little afraid of bees because their stings are very painful. What makes them almost more frightening is the knowledge that when a bee attacks a human, it is on a suicide mission. Its sting has a barb, so the bee cannot pull it out of a person's skin without fatally injuring itself. People are very rarely killed by a bee sting, but the bee dies every time.

Suicide is almost unheard of in nature, and even among social insects like bees or wasps it is unusual. The behaviour of bees is also unusual in other ways. For one thing, the bees that visit flowers (and occasionally sting people), help other members of their hive find food by passing on information about good places to collect pollen and nectar. Such cooperation is almost as rare in nature as suicide. Another unusual thing is that most bees are sterile. Bees are really very odd creatures indeed, and it is all because of the way they breed.

A hive of bees may have 100,000 individuals in it, but only one of them is capable of producing eggs, and she is known as the queen. All the others are her offspring, and the vast majority of them are the sterile females known as workers. These are the ones that gather food, feed the queen, and look after the eggs she lays. The workers are also the ones that sting any intruder who tries to steal the colony's honey store. The males are called drones, and in a colony of this size there may be about 200 of them.

The workers cannot mate and produce their own offspring, but by feeding the queen and caring for her young they can still help to pass on the family's genes. When the colony is really thriving, or when the queen is getting old, a few eggs are raised to produce new queens. The eggs themselves are just the same as the ones that normally produce workers, but they are fed extra nutritious food so that they grow into fertile queens. When a queen leaves the colony, she takes with her a swarm of workers and drones, and together they set up a new colony.

Bumblebees provide useful clues to the evolution of bee society. Colonies start each spring with a single queen building a nest, laying a few eggs and looking after them. But when they grow up, the first brood are miniatures because they had only the queen to feed them, and one bee alone cannot gather much food. The poor diet also leaves them sterile, so as workers they take over the job of caring for the next brood. Each brood is better fed than the one before, and eventually the young are so well nourished that they become fertile queens and fly off to establish new colonies.

To understand the behaviour of honeybees and bumblebees it is helpful to know a little about bee genetics, which are rather different from human genetics. A female bee is extremely closely related to her sisters. They share many more common characteristics than human sisters, and in fact they are more closely related than any two humans except identical twins. When a new queen flies from a hive to mate and set up her own colony, she is mating on behalf of all her sisters, the workers that raised her, carrying their genes on to the next generation. Because the workers cannot breed themselves, the queen does their breeding for them, and so the workers must protect her and her offspring at all costs. Even if a worker is killed while stinging an animal that invades the honey store, the sacrifice of her life is more than repaid if it means that the colony survives to continue breeding.

▶▶ Honey-bee workers feeding young and storing food in a large wild colony in a dead tree. The thousands of bees in a colony all work together because they are so closely related. The survival of the colony is far more important than the life of an individual bee.

INSTINCT AND LEARNING

In 1928, people in Southampton, England, discovered that their milk bottles were being pecked open by local birds. The principal culprits were found to be blue tits, whose agility made perching on the slippery bottles easy and whose sharp bills made short work of the bottle tops. The birds had found a new source of food and were eagerly exploiting it.

Since then, all over Britain, the birds have adopted this habit. But they have taken it a step further. Milk now comes in several different grades, identified by differently-coloured foil caps — and the birds have now learned that the creamiest milk comes in the bottles with gold tops, and so they open them first.

This curious behaviour is part instinct — part learning. The blue tit will instinctively peck at anything bright, shiny or colourful; its natural foods include insects, berries, flowers and seeds. In this case the birds learned from experience. A few pecked at the coloured milk bottle tops, discovered a new source of food, and from then on visited milk bottles regularly when feeding. The later refinement of learning the difference between bottles containing full milk and those containing semi-skimmed and skimmed milk surprised even the scientists.

▶ By instinct the Laysan albatross tries to incubate round, smooth, pale objects. These are normally its own eggs, but occasionally things can go wrong: in this case the patient bird is incubating a plastic fishing-net float.

Instinct

▶ A ten-day-old baby racoon clings desperately to a tree trunk. The climbing movements are instinctive, but it will take months of practice before the youngster can climb to the top quickly and safely like its parents and cousins.

Many animals never have the opportunity to learn anything about how they are supposed to behave as parents. They never meet their own parents, and have only fleeting contact with others of their kind. Yet these animals still have a rich repertoire of behaviour. Many solitary wasps and bees, for example, build elaborate nests that they provision with food for their young, following a series of complex actions that must somehow be programmed into their genes. Leaf-cutter bees excavate holes in the ground or in dead wood which they then line with pieces of leaf cut from selected plants. In this carefully constructed nest the female assembles a store of pollen as food for her larvae. Cicada-killer wasps build simpler nests but their instinctive behaviour is no less remarkable. Their young are fed almost exclusively on adult cicadas, paralysed by the wasp's sting and carried back to deep underground burrows.

Even animals that seem to be simple can carry out complex tasks without being taught by their parents, and this behaviour is almost entirely instinctive. But instinctive behaviour has its limitations. In particular, animals that rely on instinct can find it difficult to adapt to unusual situations. In Australia there lives a wasp that stocks its underground burrow with caterpillars for its larvae to feed on when they hatch. At the entrance to the burrow these wasps build an elaborate structure from mud pellets moulded into the shape of a smoker's pipe. The "bowl" of the pipe faces downwards, which apparently makes it difficult for other wasps to get in and steal the hoard of food in the burrow.

◀ Young herring gulls instinctively peck at the red spot on the parent's bill, and in response the adult will regurgitate a meal of partly-digested fish. The instinct is so strong that a chick will peck at a red spot painted on a cardboard cutout in the shape of a gull's bill.

The construction of this pipe is a fascinating piece of instinctive behaviour, but when an accident or an inquisitive biologist makes a hole in the stem, the problems of instinct suddenly become obvious. If the hole is small and close to the edge of the bowl, the wasp will simply repair it. But otherwise, when the wasp finds a hole in its pipe it treats the hole as the tip of the pipe. Instead of repairing the damage, it sets about building a new pipe sticking out of the side of the original one. It is as if the wasp has only one response to an opening in its mud construction and that is to build onto it. It does not have the instinct to repair it – nor the mental powers necessary to analyse the situation and decide on an appropriate course of action.

Simple animals can clearly perform complicated tasks instinctively, but any task that throws up unpredictable problems is difficult to complete simply by following a pre-programmed set of instructions.

▼ Bees are able to exploit food resources very efficiently because workers returning to the hive can tell others exactly where food is to be found. If it is closer than 50m to the hive the worker does her "round dance", running round in a circle, first clockwise and then anticlockwise (below left). If the food source is more than 50m away she performs a "figure-of-eight" dance on the vertical face of the comb. First she makes a short straight run, then she circles to the left, runs back up the straight and circles right. It is the orientation of the straight section in relation to the hive that tells other bees where the food is located. If it is vertical and directed upward, the food source is in the direction of the Sun. If it is vertical but downward, the food lies directly away from the Sun. And if it is at an angle to the vertical, that is the direction the bees must take – measuring the same angle from the Sun. The number of times the bee waggles her abdomen during the straight part of the dance also tells other bees how far away the food is.

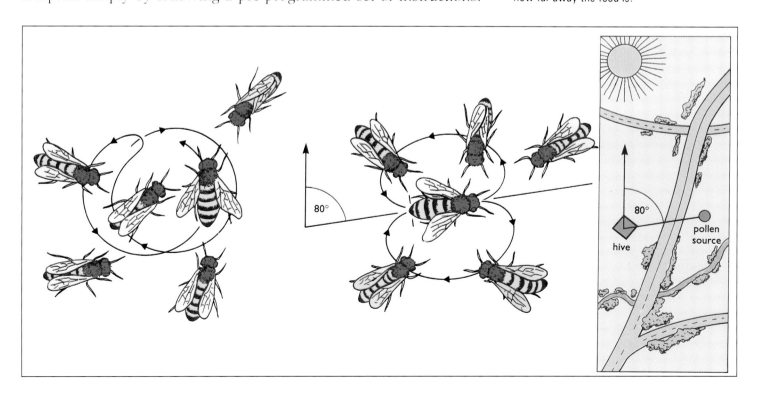

▶ Alaskan sockeye salmon fight their way upstream as they return to the river of their birth in order to spawn. Much of their migration behaviour is instinctive, but some also depends on learning. Salmon are hatched far inland, in the headwaters of freshwater rivers, but when still quite small they swim downstream and out to sea where they spend several years feeding and growing to maturity. As young fish they must learn the characteristic smell of their home river. Then, when the time comes for them to return to breed, they navigate back to the very same headwaters − literally smelling and tasting their way back home.

▲ Snow geese migrate purely by instinct, but they travel in family groups within the flock so that the young ones are able to learn the details of the journey from their parents.

Although many animals have instinctive patterns of behaviour, most also take advantage of their ability to learn. Migratory birds have an instinctive drive that tells them which way to fly, and when. Birds kept in cages away from others of their kind automatically become restless and try to take off in the direction of their migration route when the time comes, which means that they instinctively know which way to fly. The information is programmed into the genes they inherited from their parents. But birds equipped only with the simple instinct to "head south when winter comes" would get lost far more often than they do.

In practice, birds learn to correct their flight direction in strong winds even before they begin their migration. Most birds also make their first journey south in the company of others that have made the trip before. Ducks and geese often travel in family units, while many other species migrate in large flocks made up of both first-year birds and adults. By taking birds from one area and moving them to another, scientists have shown that birds with an instinct to migrate in one direction will learn from adults a completely different migration route. In this way, learning modifies and improves the underlying instinct. When an individual turns up in totally the wrong place, it is often followed by hundreds or even thousands of dedicated bird-watchers. The reason why these occasional visitors draw such an audience is that they appear so rarely. The combination of instinct, learning and experience is remarkably efficient.

Learning Before Birth

◀ Gamekeepers have known for many years that the birds they raise in incubators are much more stupid than wild birds. They seem to have no idea how to hide from hawks and foxes, and many are killed before they reach maturity. In the wild, the mother teaches her chicks which other animals are dangerous by making a special call signalling them to keep still and quiet. But this is not the whole story. If they are to learn these lessons when they have hatched, birds like these freshly hatched silver pheasants must first have heard these warning calls while they were still inside the egg.

One subject that has obsessed artists for almost 2,000 years is the Madonna and Child. Michelangelo, Leonardo and Rembrandt all painted pictures of the scene, and most of the less well known artists have had a try at it. In almost all of these pictures the mother is holding the baby in the same way, with its head against her left breast. Of course it is not only the Madonna who holds her baby like this. Most women, whether they are right or left handed, cradle their baby in the same way.

Before it is born, a baby spends months inside its mother's womb and there it hears the workings of her body. One sound it hears day and night is the beating of its mother's heart. Once it is born, a baby's life changes completely: it is faced with a barrage of new sights, tastes and smells. Although a mother is seldom consciously aware of it, by cradling the baby in her arms she places its ear next to her heart. Warm and secure against its mother's left breast, the baby hears a sound that is familiar and reassuring.

Tape-recordings of a mother's heart-beat can often help to calm her new-born baby. Unfortunately for parents, however, the tape-recorded heart-beat does not continue to calm a baby for very long. It soon realizes that it is not getting the real thing!

A baby begins to learn about its world even before it is born. As well as the sound of its mother's heart, a new-born baby can be soothed by the sound of her voice, which it also learned in the womb and recognizes the moment it is born. Even the theme music from a soap opera that the mother watched regularly while she was pregnant may soothe a fretful baby. Long before it is born the baby learns the everyday sounds of its surroundings and immediately shows interest when it hears them again. Perhaps just as importantly it can be ready with a shriek of alarm when faced with anything usual.

How much other animals learn from the sounds they hear in their mother's womb is a mystery. This is hardly surprising since doctors only recently realized that babies could hear while still in the womb. Before this discovery was made, anyone trying to study how much animals can learn before they are born would probably have been thought a little crazy, or at least mildly eccentric.

Imprinting

On the first day of spring a photographer on almost every local newspaper is sent out to find a suitably cheerful picture. If the town is under feet of snow or the crocuses in the local park are drowning, a good alternative is to find a farm where a clutch of goslings or ducklings has been raised away from their mother. "Best of Friends" the caption says, and the picture shows the brood snuggled up with a cat, a goat or a pet rabbit. The caption even seems to be true, because the young birds actually do follow the other animals about.

In the wild, goslings do not usually end up forming close relationships with animals like cats. The unusual behaviour is a result of the unnatural conditions in which the goslings are raised. Only hours after they hatch, wild goslings leave their nest and begin to feed themselves, but they do not set off into the world totally alone. The family sticks together, with the parents leading the young to good feeding places and protecting them from the weather and from predators. For this to work, the goslings have got to do their part; they have to stick close to their parents.

When they hatch, goslings are equipped with many instincts. They can peck, feed and walk, but instinct alone cannot tell them how to identify their mother. So, they instinctively follow the nearest large, moving object, which in the wild is always their mother. Within hours of hatching they can distinguish her from any other goose, a neat trick since to human eyes all geese look much the same. From then on, they follow her through thick and thin.

This learning process is called "imprinting", and it is special in several ways. It is an unusually fast and thorough learning process which takes place at a critical time in a gosling's life, just after it hatches. Once learned, the lesson can never be unlearned, and a clutch of goslings that makes the mistake of following a pet cat or rabbit on the day that they hatch will always regard that animal as their mother. For male goslings the mistake is a total disaster, because imprinting determines not only what they recognize as their mother, but also what they recognize as a female of their kind. If a male gosling becomes imprinted on a cat or rabbit at birth, when it becomes an adult it will attempt to mate with a cat or rabbit and will completely ignore any geese that are around.

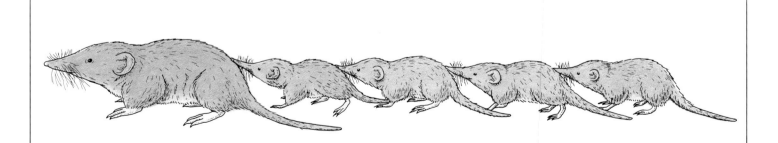

▲ When young shrews are old enough to leave the nest, but still too young and vulnerable to survive alone, they form into a line behind the mother and each one takes a firm grip on the rump of the one in front. Securely tied together in this way, the youngsters are taken on a tour of the big wide world beyond the safety of the nest burrow. The animals keep such a firm grip with their sharp teeth that the whole "caravan" can be picked up by lifting the mother from the ground.

◀ These gosling chicks brought up by a broody hen will be firmly imprinted on their foster mother. When the males from the clutch reach breeding age they will court hens instead of geese, so although imprinting may ensure the survival of a few individuals, in evolutionary terms it is a disaster: these males will never produce another generation of geese.

It is not only ducks and geese that learn to identify their mother in this way. In the same farmyard there may be sheep that were bottle-fed as lambs. Such lambs grow up to be a nuisance because, like goslings, they follow their foster-mothers everywhere – including into the house and out onto the roads. This is one reason why most farmers prefer to foster orphaned lambs on other sheep rather than raise them by hand. But fostering orphaned lambs is not easy, because in sheep the recognition of the lamb by the mother is just as important. During a two-hour period after she gives birth, the mother quickly learns the smell of her own lamb and from then on refuses to allow any others to suckle. In order to persuade a sheep to foster a lamb that is not her own it must first be smeared with blood from the afterbirth of her own lamb. The practice sounds gory, but it is essential that the new lamb smells right to the sheep if it is to be accepted as one of her own.

Learning About Food

▶ A young spider monkey from South America drinks nectar from a balsa flower. As the young monkey grows, it learns about such unlikely sources of food from its mother, and from other members of the troop.

For roughly 1,000 years, a small group of people in the south of Holland made their living in a most peculiar way. Every autumn they built themselves small shelters out in the fields, and on top of each shelter they put a cage containing a bird called a red-backed shrike. In front of the shelter was a complicated arrangement of poles, nets and pigeons on pieces of string. Their signal to start work came when the shrike gave its alarm call because that told them that their quarry was in sight. With great skill they then pulled the various strings, and eventually ended up capturing their prize – a spitting, pecking, clawing, adult peregrine falcon which they could sell to a falconer for a great deal of money.

The reason why falconers were prepared to pay so much for birds caught in this way, rather than follow the easier and cheaper course of taking a chick from a peregrine nest, was that birds caught in the wild are always better hunters. Birds taken from the nest would hunt, because they do so instinctively, but wild-caught birds have learned the most successful ways of catching their prey. A peregrine's survival in the wild depends on its skill in hunting, and it learns some of that skill from its parents.

Predators are not all taught how to hunt by their parents. A praying mantis is a very effective predator which feeds by catching other insects, grabbing them suddenly in its barbed front legs. Almost immediately after a mantis hatches from its egg it sets to work hunting in just the same way as its parents. The young insect never meets its parents, so they certainly never teach it anything about hunting. The behaviour is entirely instinctive, and very successful. Despite this, a praying mantis can learn, and in particular it is likely to learn to avoid certain foul-tasting insects that appear to be easily caught meals.

When animals spend time with their parents after birth, they can learn a great deal. They can learn about good places to look for food, and good sorts of food to eat. A farmyard hen, for example, teaches these things to her chicks. The chicks feed themselves, but they learn *where* to look for food from the mother hen. Young chicks start by just pecking at anything small that is clearly a different colour from the background. In this way they learn slowly, but the hen also helps by feeding her chicks occasionally. When she finds a particularly tasty morsel, she holds it in her beak and makes a croaky noise. The chicks quickly come scuttling up to her, and they learn to recognize the little snacks that she gives them.

Most bird or mammal predators go beyond the mother hen's simple teaching and actively help the young learn to catch food. Birds of prey feed their chicks at the nest, but once the young fledge they often have to chase their mother as she flies along carrying their food. When she drops the food for them to catch, they must practise all the dazzling flying skills they will need when they begin to hunt on their own.

Many animals learn by watching others perform, which has allowed some unusual sorts of behaviour to spread very quickly. Instinctive behaviour is programmed into an animal's genes, and can only be inherited by its offspring. Behaviour that is learned can often be acquired by all the animals in a group, including animals that are not even related. Within a year of birth, young macaques have already learned what is good to eat. The infant monkeys do this by watching their mothers, by catching and tasting pieces that fall into her lap as she feeds, and by picking bits right out of her mouth with their hands.

As they grow, young macaques add to their knowledge of food by learning from their playmates, and it is usually these same playful youngsters that are the first to discover a new source of food. When a troop of macaques in Japan were first given sweets, none of them recognized them as food. Eventually a two-year-old tried eating them, and the habit began to spread. First to learn were her playmates and her mother, followed by the adult males who spent a lot of time with the youngsters. Mothers quickly passed on the new information to their other offspring, and so within a litte more than a year, most members of the troop had learned that sweets were good to eat.

▲ A young North American brown bear watches closely as its mother catches salmon. This is a crucial time for the cub, because as well as learning what is good to eat, it must also learn how to catch it.

Avoiding Predators

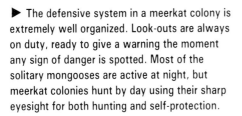

▶ The defensive system in a meerkat colony is extremely well organized. Look-outs are always on duty, ready to give a warning the moment any sign of danger is spotted. Most of the solitary mongooses are active at night, but meerkat colonies hunt by day using their sharp eyesight for both hunting and self-protection.

A single pair of sparrowhawks will kill about ten small birds every day during the summer in order to feed their chicks. Most of the birds brought back to the nest will be young ones that have only just learned to fly. These little birds are killed before they even manage to breed, which means that they really have to be written off as failures. Most animals are under pressure like this, which is why helping youngsters avoid predators is a top priority for animals that look after their offspring in any way.

The most obvious thing that parents can do to protect their offspring is to defend them directly, and most animals do this if they can. Geese may appear to be "harmless" grass-eaters but they can give a very nasty peck, and they do just that to any predator that threatens their eggs or chicks. This type of defence is so widespread that it is true of almost all domesticated animals, a fact that makes a vet's life both hazardous and humorous to read about. By attacking a predator, the parents protect their offspring directly and at the same time teach them to identify their enemies.

Many animals, particularly birds, appear to teach their young about predators even when they are not under threat. When a sparrowhawk alights in a garden, the resident birds might be expected to flee, or dive for cover, but they do no such thing. Instead, they begin screeching and chattering their alarm calls, diving and circling around the intruder.

This "mobbing" behaviour carries little risk, because a perched sparrowhawk has little chance of catching a bird in flight. Eventually the noise and harassment will force the hawk to settle elsewhere, but the main effect of all the commotion is to teach the young birds to identify a dangerous enemy.

Some animals need to be taught what a predator looks like, while others know their enemies instinctively. Even so, they can refine this instinct by learning. Several species of monkey are born with an instinctive fear of snakes, but apparently learn from their mothers which are dangerous and which can be ignored. When it sees a snake, an infant will scream with terror, but if the snake is harmless the mother will pay no obvious attention to her infant, except perhaps to keep a foot on its tail to make sure it stays close to her. If the snake is poisonous, the mother will quickly grab her youngster and scamper to safety. The infant's instinctive response keeps it out of danger, but learning exactly what to look out for will save it time and energy in later life.

Because the monkey's recognition of snakes is learned, it is flexible. If a troop finds itself in a new area where the snakes have different markings, it will not take long for at least some of them to learn which ones are dangerous, and this information can then be passed on to the next generation. Until they become familiar with their new surroundings, the monkeys can fall back on their instinctive fear of snakes and run from anything that slithers.

▲ Many small flocking birds will distract predators and confuse them by swirling around them in a screaming mob. In this photograph, a young steppe eagle and a great spotted eagle are being mobbed by red-wattled lapwings. An added effect of mobbing behaviour may be to help young birds learn what dangerous predators look like, by drawing attention to them.

Learning Through Play

Some adults seem to spend a lot of their time trying to stop children playing. They are usually people who work very hard themselves and think of play as being the opposite of work and therefore a waste of time. For humans, work is a way of getting food to eat and a comfortable place to live, and like humans, animals must spend time doing the same things. In spite of this, children carry on playing, and so do other young animals. It is quite possible to keep both a small child and a kitten amused for hours with a piece of ribbon. The kitten pounces on the ribbon, throws its end up in the air, bites it, holds it in its paws and then ambushes it from behind a chair leg. The child just has to keep twitching the ribbon and the kitten will go on playing this game for ages.

Lion cubs in the wild play in much the same way as kittens in the living room. The cubs stalk their mother's twitching tail and pounce on each other in mock ambush. In fact, the young of many meat-eating mammals do the same thing: they have play fights, and suddenly by using that phrase "play fight" the animal's play takes on a new importance. This is no longer just play for its own sake: it is also training for the future.

▲ The playful antics of lion cubs seem as innocent as the play of any young animal, yet there is a serious purpose behind it all. The stalking, pouncing and swiping blows of the tiny claws will very soon develop into the deadly weapons of a powerful hunter.

Many of the skills that animals learn during play can be seen as practice for something, but hunting is the skill that is most obviously practised in play. Hunting is often a very complicated performance for a sophisticated predator because each hunt is unique. It calls for precise movements, timing, and even planning. Skill like that cannot all be instinctive, it has to be learned. Experience is what counts, but animals can gain experience by playing – without injuring themselves as they almost certainly would if their first forays into the world of hunting were directed at real prey animals.

Elephant groups are led by a dominant female, and within the group there is a definite order of seniority among all the other females. In social animals such as elephants, the playful games of the young are an important part of learning the rules of the society they will later join as adults.

During play a young animal is mainly teaching itself. An adult lioness will play with her cubs, but she does not have to show them how to stalk each other, nor does a kitten have to be shown how to chase a ribbon. Instinctively they pounce on almost anything that moves, but through practising their stalking and pouncing skills, they learn the movements and tactics that will be important when they begin to hunt for themselves.

Hunting may be the most obvious skill practised in play, but it is far from being the only one. Lambs and goat kids play endlessly, although as adults they will never hunt anything more challenging than a clump of grass. But for these youngsters too, play is an important part of learning. Sheep and goats are naturally hill and mountain animals. Dancing, chasing and skipping all exercise young legs and develop a sure-footed sense of balance that will keep them safe on the steepest crags. Play fighting games like "King of the Castle" are practice for the battles to come in years ahead when the males will have to fight for the chance to mate.

Children's play is perhaps not so very different from that of other animals. Climbing trees, catching flies, making miniature gardens and building camps are not the most obvious training for the adult world, but the physical coordination and planning involved is not really so different from that required of a lorry driver or businessman. In fact, company executives have recently taken to fighting mock battles in the gardens of large country estates as one way of improving their planning and management skills.

What we know about animals shows us that playing is a very good way of learning, so maybe one of the best ways for humans to learn is by playing. Children find playing is fun, and hardly notice that they are also learning at the same time. Most humans continue to play games long after they have become adults, which is not true of any other animal, and perhaps that is because we humans rely so much on our ability to learn. Those few adults who still feel that play is the opposite of work, and that work should be boring, should watch lion cubs chasing grasshoppers across the African savanna. It is impossible not to feel that the cubs are having a great game. But go back and watch the same cubs a few years later when they have reached maturity and the skills they learned with the grasshoppers are being put to deadly effect.

Learning to be Parents

It is always exciting to watch birds at the nest. The parents' actions are so quick and precise, and they seem to know just what they must do to rear their young ones successfully. But the cuckoo makes a mockery of it all. How can a pair of reed warblers feeding a cuckoo possibly mistake that great ugly squawking intruder for a nest full of their own tiny chicks?

Breeding birds show both the strength and the limitation of instinctive behaviour. Almost all the things that reed warblers do instinctively while raising their young are designed to help the young survive and thrive. But the cuckoo cleverly steals the hard work of the reed warblers for its own ends. The reed warblers with one big ugly chick in their nest instead of three or four small ones continue with the same instinctive behaviour, feeding and cleaning up after the imposter – and that is where instinct lets them down. For an animal to cope with the unusual, it has to develop its own individual behaviour patterns, and it can only do that by learning.

If being a parent involves entirely predictable tasks, instinctive behaviour is very effective. But if parenthood is a variable job, instinct is much less useful. Animals whose lives are complex and unpredictable must learn how to be parents, and the best way of learning that is from their own parents. Young monkeys, for example, stay with their parents and learn from them how to find food and how to behave in monkey society. They may also learn some of the skills of

◀ Wolves have a great deal to learn if they are to survive, and they can only learn within the security of the pack. Only the dominant male and female mate and produce young, but all the pack members help to raise the cubs and to protect them as they learn the rules of society and the techniques of survival and hunting.

being a parent by practising on younger relations. They learn how to handle a youngster, to groom it, and to keep it out of danger – and they learn those things from the way their own parents treat them. They will not use what they have learned for a while, perhaps for several years, but what they learn when they are young can make them successful parents when they grow up. If a monkey learns to find food it will survive, but only if it learns how to look after young ones will it be able to breed successfully.

◀ A dark-plumaged immature albatross joins in as an adult pair perform their courtship ritual. An albatross pair will usually remain together for life, and even though it will be several years before this young male seeks a mate, when the time comes it will be important for him to establish a strong, permanent pair-bond with her.

Human Learning

A bear makes an interesting comparison with a human. The bear can overtake a running man. It can swim faster than a human, it can climb trees faster, and it is much stronger. It can catch a human, knock him down, and tear him to pieces. But humans can design houses that even bears cannot break into, and have invented weapons such as spears and rifles, against which even the most powerful bear is defenceless.

The things that humans are particularly good at are thinking and inventing, and both these abilities are the result of our amazing capacity for learning. No animal can learn as much as a human, and no animal can use its experience in such a variety of ways. However, while we can invent computers and understand ecology, we also invent guns and chemicals, and then hunt and poison animals to the brink of extinction. We are very good at learning – but we do also make mistakes when deciding how to use this special talent.

Almost from birth a baby starts to learn about other people. It learns to smile, and it learns that other people smile back when it does so. It learns to make noises and to control the noises it makes, and then it learns that noises like "Ma-Ma" or "Da-Da" produce a terrific response in the people round it. They jump up and down, smile and talk to it, so the baby does it again.

▶ Children play for fun, but they also learn a great deal about the real world from their make-believe games. It is much safer to test things out with toys or imagination than to tackle real situations too soon and ill-prepared.

By the age of three, children have generally learned to use a language. They can talk about what they are doing, what they want, and about the things they have experienced. They manage to learn grammar, so that as well as knowing what words mean they can make up sentences that describe something totally new. These first steps in understanding the world can be comical. A toddler who has learned to recognize the family cat as "pussy" but who has never seen an alsatian dog might turn to its mother and ask uncertainly "big pussy?" The chance to make mistakes without danger is perhaps one of the most important things about learning.

◀ Imagination and ingenuity know no bounds. These Eritrean children living in a refugee camp have no manufactured toys, but have made their own from whatever materials they could find around the camp.

Language is not inherited from a child's parents. Instead, the child learns its language by listening to the people around it. Children who are separated from their parents at birth and are adopted by people from another country may grow up to speak a language that their parents never even knew existed. Nobody is totally sure how toddlers learn to talk, but they obviously learn by listening to other people and by talking.

What we inherit from our parents is not language itself but the ability to learn. Because our language is learned, and learned from many different people, it can develop very much faster than if it were something we inherited. A new human invention can immediately be given a name and its parts described so that people who have never even seen it can put it together and use it. Isolated groups of chimpanzees and monkeys learn to use tools for cracking open nuts or for fishing termites from their holes, but these skills rarely spread to neighbouring groups. Each group must invent its tricks for itself. But thousands of years ago, isolated groups of humans all across Europe and the Middle East were using similar tools to harvest wheat and to kill game. Our language, and our ability to learn from each other, have enabled us to pass on our tricks for survival to many other people, and to learn from them. Our imagination then enables us to invent yet more tricks to make our tools ever more efficient.

▲ Games like blind-man's-buff are fun in any language, and as they play these children will be learning about themselves, about their companions and about their society.

The ability to communicate with each other makes humans uniquely social creatures. We even learn about ourselves from other people. We learn how other people expect us to behave, and we learn what other people think of us. As we grow up, we continue to change the way in which we behave to try and make sure that the people we like to be with will enjoy being with us.

In most of our behaviour, we humans are more variable than other animals, and the same is true of the way we behave as parents. In some societies, men take virtually no part in bringing up their children, while in others it is more usual for both men and women to share the work. Children may be treated as easily exploited slaves, or as fragile creatures who have to be protected.

This variety of behaviour and culture is confusing, and some people have tried hard to explain it by looking at the way animals behave. By carefully choosing their examples, some people have argued that it is natural for men to behave like stags and keep a large harem, while others claim that it is natural for both parents to have only one partner and to help in looking after their young since that is what most birds do. None of these arguments do anything to help us understand ourselves

or to justify our behaviour, for two reasons. First, all animals face different environments, challenges and problems in the struggle to survive from day to day and from generation to generation. Animal life is so wonderfully varied that we can find examples of almost every kind of behaviour. Second, and perhaps even more important, we humans have a choice in how we behave. Although our genes and our culture might make us act in one way rather than another, people can and often do decide to live very differently from the way their parents lived, and even to adopt the lifestyle of a totally different culture.

Animals enrich our lives with their song, their colours, their grace and their variety. They are a source of awe, wonder, humour and sometimes fear. We use them for food and clothing, as beasts of burden and as pets. But the animals can tell us little about how we should live our lives as husbands, wives or parents. We can only marvel at the perfection with which they adapt to their own environment, and search elsewhere for the answers to our deeper questions.

▲ Father and daughter may find their way on the map together, but the most he can do for her future life is to teach her the basic rules of survival and try to guide her in the right direction. The rest of the journey through adult life will be up to her.

Glossary

adaptation A part of the form or behaviour of an organism that makes it well suited to its environment. For example, the long neck of a giraffe is an adaptation that allows it to feed from tall trees.

amphibian The animal group that includes frogs, toads and newts. All have a moist glandular skin, and gills at some stage in their development. Most of them spend part of their life in water and part on land.

antibodies Proteins in the body that react with foreign chemicals to make them harmless.

camouflage A disguise that is the result of a creature having the same colour and pattern as the background against which it is seen.

cell The microscopic structural unit from which all living organisms are built.

chromosomes The thread-like structures seen in the nucleus as a cell divides. Chromosomes are composed of DNA bound together with proteins.

dominant A dominant animal in a group can take resources like food and mates from others.

ecology The study of the way in which an organism relates to its surroundings.

evolution The slow process by which plants and animals change over succeeding generations as they adapt to their changing surroundings.

fertilization The process by which egg and sperm join together.

genes The basic units of inheritance. Each gene controls the production of one particular protein.

genetics The study of the way in which genes are inherited.

gestation The period in mammals between fertilization and birth.

hermaphrodite An animal or plant that produces both eggs *and* sperm in the same individual. In synchronous hermaphrodites, the organism produces both eggs and sperm at the same time. In sequential hermaphrodites, the organism 'changes sex' producing first one, and then the other.

hierarchy A form of social structure. In a hierarchy, one animal is dominant to all others. The next animal down the hierarchy is subordinate to this one, and dominates all the rest, and so on until at the bottom, one animal is dominated by all the others.

hormones Chemical messengers released into the blood-stream that act on tissues elsewhere in the body.

hybrid A plant or animal resulting from the mating of two different species.

incubation The process by which birds keep their eggs at the ideal temperature for growth and development.

infertile Unable to produce offspring.

larva The immature stage of an animal that is markedly different from the adult, e.g. caterpillars, tadpoles.

mammal A warm-blooded animal that cares for its young by providing milk from mammary glands.

marsupial A mammal in which the female's mammary glands are enclosed in a pouch, e.g. kangaroos, opossums.

mature Fully grown and developed, and so ready to reproduce.

metamorphosis A substantial change in an animal's structure during development, e.g. from a tadpole to a frog, or from a caterpillar to a butterfly.

monotreme A small and unusual group of mammals which lay eggs. Includes the echidnas and the duck-billed platypus.

natural selection Of all the individuals in a single generation, only a few will survive to breed. The theory of natural selection is that these survivors will be the ones that are best-suited to the present conditions.

nucleus The structure within a cell that contains the chromosomes.

nymph The immature stage in those insects in which juveniles are relatively similar to the adult form, e.g. in mayflies.

parasite An organism that lives in or on another organism from which it obtains food, shelter or other essentials.

parthenogenesis The production of young from eggs without fertilization.

period Shedding the lining of the womb to produce a bloody discharge from the vagina.

placenta The organ that joins the foetus to the wall of its mother's womb in all mammals except marsupials and monotremes.

pollen The tiny male reproductive bodies produced by flowering plants, which contain the plants' equivalent of sperm.

predator An animal that hunts other animals as a source of food.

prey An animal that is killed as a source of food.

pupa A stage in insect life-cycles when the larva is enclosed in a protective case and changes into a new form.

rut The period of maximum sexual activity in male animals, particularly applied to deer.

sexual selection When an animal is ready to breed, it must first find a mate. Animals choose their mates, often accepting one and rejecting others. The theory of sexual selection is that some forms will die out because they are less good at finding mates.

social insects Insects that live in colonies with a division of labour and in which many of the members never produce young of their own.

species A group of similar animals or plants which can actually or potentially interbreed with each other.

subordinate An animal that is dominated. (See dominant).

territory The area defended by an animal before and during the breeding season.

twins Two offspring born at the same time to the same mother. Identical twins are the result of a single fertilized egg splitting in two early in development. Since they contain the same genetic material they are usually identical in appearance. Non-identical twins are the result of two different eggs being fertilized at the same time, and are no more alike than normal brothers or sisters.

virus A minute parasite consisting of a core of genetic material surrounded by a protein coat. Viruses can only reproduce by hijacking the machinery of a plant or animal cell to copy their own genetic material.

Index

Page numbers in *italics*
represent illustrations

Acknowledgments

FRONT AND BACK COVER:

All photographs from Bruce Coleman: White-tailed doe (Leonard Lee Rue III), Asian elephant (Dieter & Mary Plage), chimpanzee (Helmut Albrecht), bottle-nosed dolphins (Jeff Foott), silver pheasant chicks (Jane Burton)

IN TEXT:

Ardea London: 22 (Masahiro Iijima), 97 (D. W. Greenslade), 145 (F. Colett)

Charles Arneson: 39 below

Chris Catton/Green Films: 52, 86, 152

Bruce Coleman: 7 (Jeff Foott), 23 (Michael Viard), 26 (Jen & Des Bartlett), 36–7 (N. Fenech), 39 top (Jen & Des Bartlett), 40, 44 & 45 (Jeff Foott), 46 (Jen & Des Bartlett), 47 (Frieder Sauer), 50 & 51 (David & Carol Hughes), 53 (Dieter & Mary Plage), 54 (Frieder Sauer), 61 (Udo Hirsch), 62 (Peter Ward), 63 (Gordon Langsbury), 66–7 (K. Wothe), 77 (Owen Tomalin), 79 (Frans Lanting), 83 (Jeff Foott), 87 (Erwin & Peggy Bauer), 88–9 (Hans Reinhard), 92–3 (Dieter & Mary Plage), 95 (Jen & Des Bartlett), 107 (Michael Viard), 108 (Frieder Sauer), 115 (Carol Hughes), 117 (Jane Burton), 118 (Helmut Albrecht), 119 (Kim Taylor), 126 top (Carl Wallace), 134 (Erwin & Peggy Bauer), 140 (Jane Burton), 142 (George McCarthy), 143 below (Leonard Lee Rue III), 144 (M.P. Price), 146 & 154 (Dieter & Mary Plage), 155 (Jeff Foott), 157 (Erwin & Peggy Bauer), 161 (Frieder Sauer), 163 (Jane Burton), 165 (Frans Lanting), 166 (Leonard Lee Rue III), 168–9 (Dr Eckart Pott), 170 (Jeff Foott), 171 (Jane Burton), 175 (Leonard Lee Rue III), 178 (Günter Ziesler), 179 (Christian Zuber), 180–1 (Günter Ziesler).

Sally & Richard Greenhill: 15, 16, 24, 25, 55, 185.

The Hutchison Library: 10, 17, 31, 49 (Liba Taylor), 60, 150 (Nancy Durrell McKenna), 183 (Sarah Errington), 184.

NHPA: 2–3 (Orion Press), 94 (G.I. Bernard), 149 (Stephen Dalton), 173 (Joe B. Blossom).

Network: 182 (Steve King).

Oxford Scientific Films: 1 (G.I. Bernard), 4–5 (Michael Fogden), 8–9 (Stouffer Prod. Ltd), 21 (Ray Richardson), 27 (Andrew Plumtre), 29 (Bob Frederick), 33, 34 (G.I. Bernard), 38 (Michael Fogden), 41 (P. Kent), 59 (G.I. Bernard), 64–5 (Andrew Plumtre), 68 (H.L. Fox), 71 (C.M. Perrins), 72 (Michael Fogden), 74–5 (Partridge Productions), 76 (Richard Packwood), 80 & 81 (Tony Allen), 85 (Kathie Atkinson), 90 (Babs & Bert Wells), 91 (Rudie Kuiter), 98 & 100–1 (G.I. Bernard), 103 (Barrie Watts), 104–5 (Peter Parks), 106 (John Cheverton), 109 (Phil Devries), 110 (G.I. Bernard), 113 (Kim Westerskov), 116 (John Cooke), 120 (David Shale), 121 & 123 (Michael Fogden), 125 (London Scientific Films), 126 below (J.A.L. Cooke), 126–7 top (Rudie Kuiter), 127 top (Breck P. Kent), 128, 129 & 131 (Michael Fogden), 130 (Rodger Jackman), 132 (M.A. Chapell), 133 (Doug Allen), 135 (A.G. Wells), 136–7 (Kathie Atkinson), 139 (Kim Westerskov), 141 (Tony Allen), 143 top (Richard Packwood), 147 (Mantis Wildlife Films), 151 (G.I. Bernard), 153 (J.A.L. Cooke), 156 (David Macdonald), 158–9 (Michael Fogden), 160 (Michael Leach), 167 (Ben Osborne), 174 (Michael Fogden), 176 (David Mcdonald), 181 (Ben Osborne).

Planet Earth Pictures/Seaphot: 42–3 (Jonathon Scott), 65 (Nick Greaves), 67 (Richard Matthews), 69 (Peter Scownes), 70 (David Kjaer), 84–5 (K. & K. Ammann), 96–7 (Carl Roessler), 99 (Norbert Wu), 126–7 below (Ken Lucas), 148 (Richard Matthews), 177 (Sue Earle).

Science Photo Library: 13 (Petit Format), 35 (David Scharf).

Frank Spooner Pictures: 14 (Gamma).

Sally Anne Thompson/Animal Photography: 78.

Dr Merlin D. Tuttle, Bat Conservation International Inc., Austin, Texas: 56–7.

Walker Art Gallery, Liverpool. Courtesy of the National Museums and Galleries on Merseyside: 18.